To Faye,

Hope you enjoy the stories of an old County boy.

Roy A Crump Jr

Dec 9, 2009

Between the Creeks

Between the Creeks

My Sapony Adventures

BY ROY A. COOPER JR.

Tales of a boy
and the family and friends
who shaped his life

Foreword by
Attorney General Roy Cooper and
Judge Pell Cooper

CHAPEL HILL
PRESS, INC.

Map courtesy of Karen S. Hill.
Jacket photographs by Michael Brantley.

ISBN: 978-1-59715-054-5
Library of Congress Catalog Number: 2008928218

First Printing

Along Old Bailey Highway, State Road 1001, three miles south of Nashville, the county seat of Nash County, North Carolina, lies the peaceful community of Elm Grove. This neighborhood is bordered on the north by Little Sapony Creek and on the south by Big Sapony, named in honor of the Saponi Indian tribe of central North Carolina. Between, around, and in these two creeks is where I played out the adventures I have described in the stories you are about to read.

To my daughters-in-law,
Meredith and Kristin;
and to my granddaughters,
Marelle, Hilary, Natalie, and Claire.

They have never known the country life.

CONTENTS

FOREWORD

Our parents, Roy A. Cooper Jr., and Beverly B. Cooper, have played the most significant role in shaping us. With their incredible power of persuasion and teamwork as parents, they encouraged, helped, and challenged us. They taught our Sunday school classes, coached our baseball teams, and made us practice piano. They pushed us academically. They worked us hard on the farm. They taught us respect for nature and for other people. They loved us.

As adults and parents ourselves, we still treasure our relationship with Dad and Mom. We still look to them for advice and help. Hardly a day goes by that we don't talk with them, not out of obligation, but because we truly love them and enjoy our conversations.

Dad and Mom value the past, as is evident from this book. But they revel in the present. They are eager to learn the latest technology, try the newest health food, and drive the most efficient hybrid car. They open their minds to new ideas. So we weren't surprised when they teamed up on a book.

Dad wrote. Mom edited. They both worded and reworded. And the final product is a collection of tales you'll identify with and enjoy. With Dad's descriptive prose, we can taste the ham biscuits and fried chicken that our grandmother cooked for us just as she did for our dad when he was a boy.

These stories show what makes our dad tick. Outside faith and family, a quality education has always been Dad's top goal for us. From the time we went to school he expected us to perform well, and to keep it up through graduate school. When we were young, he gave us the vocabulary tests in the back of the World Book Encyclopedia. When we weren't studying, he demanded to know why. Like his parents in the chapters "Spare the Rod" and "Daddy," our dad earnestly taught us the critical importance of school success.

Dad's zest for education and learning runs through all these tales. He knew that diplomas and degrees could get us successful professions. But he wanted our quest for knowledge to last a lifetime, just as it has for him since reading those 1934 *National Geographic*s with good neighbor Van Watson. Dad has never stopped reading, traveling, and learning.

Dad's fascination always beats fear when it comes to nature. We've seen him stare down an angry hornets' nest, poisonous snakes, and a snorting, aggressive bull. Dad had never told us about his ingenious trick for catching wild bees, but when we read his "Peach Trees and Honeybees" we realized that he has always had that kind of courage.

We always knew that Dad needed his time alone when we were kids. Here he shows why he cherishes time for himself, particularly on the farm and in the woods. The chapter "Alone but Never Lonely" shows how he learned to use nature to entertain himself.

Dad stressed to us from birth the importance of giving to the community. He's worked in political campaigns for candidates he believes in, and he's always had a hand in public policy. Although Dad went about it with less bravado than Big Daddy Clark, we can see from that chapter how his grandfather, Will Clark, sparked his love of the political arena.

People tend to follow Dad's quiet and persuasive example. Leaders succeed in different ways, and this book shows how Dad's passionate determination, kindness, preparation and charisma were formed by relationships with young friends, adult neighbors, and family.

You'll enjoy this collection of boyhood stories from our dad, whether you know him or not. There's still a lot for all of us to learn there "between the creeks."

Roy A. Cooper III
Pell C. Cooper

Between the Creeks

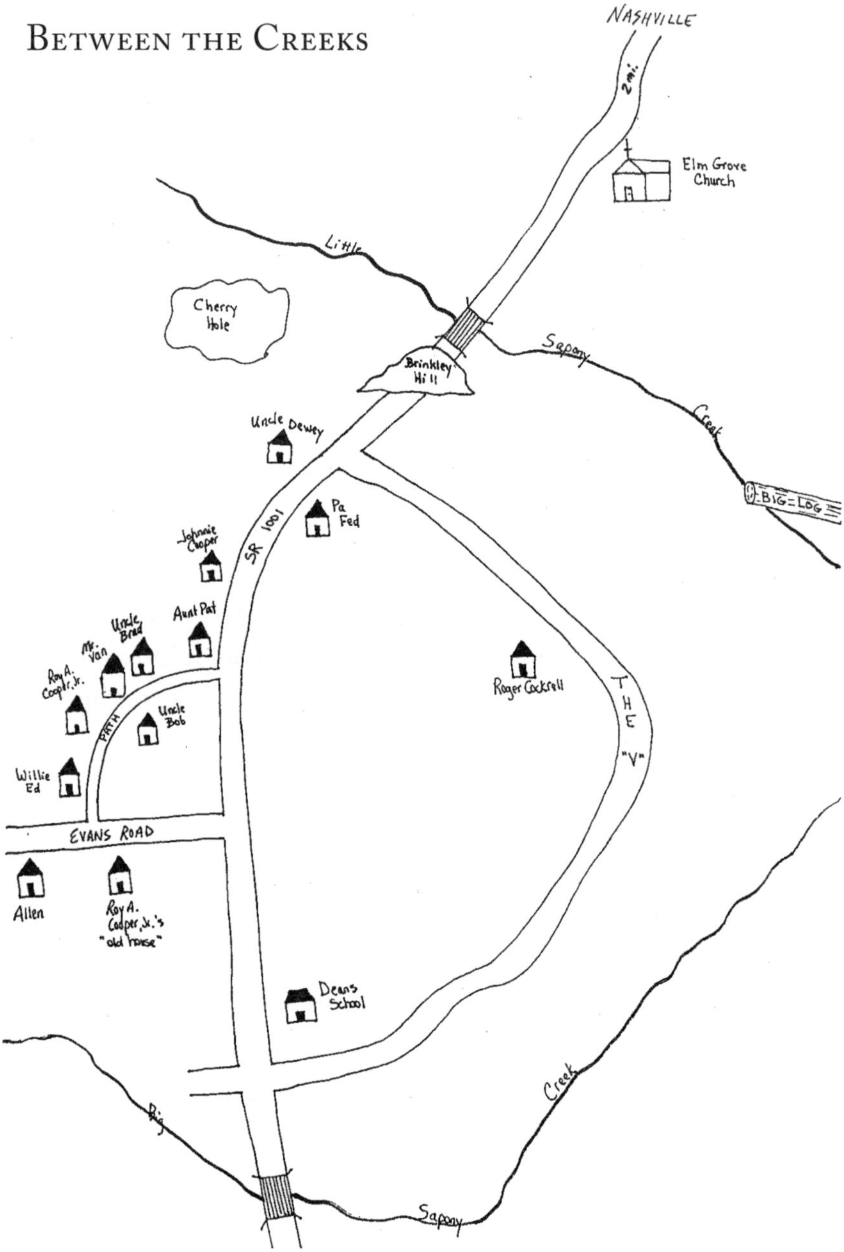

PROLOGUE

NOTHING UNUSUAL about me ... well, maybe. I was an only child, named Roy but called Tommy until my college days, brought up in a community where everyone I knew had brothers and sisters.

I believe someone said that when Mark Twain was born a shooting star was seen over his home. Well, heck, I was born on March 13, 1927, during the Big Snow. My daddy rode a horse from our farm to Nashville three miles away. Daddy said, "The snow was up to the horse's belly; we could hardly make it." I'd like to think that Mark Twain and I had something in common: natural phenomena at the times of our births and, of course, writing.

My life has been good. I married Beverly Batchelor, the perfect girl for me; made lots of friends; developed some influence in Nash and the surrounding counties; and became the father of an attorney general and a district court judge.

My wife, two sons, two daughters-in-law, and I all have graduate degrees. Our oldest granddaughter is in her second year of law school, and the other three granddaughters love to learn. My daddy would be proud!

I had a lot of fun writing the stories you are about to read. I hope you have fun reading them.

CHAPTER ONE

Life Begins

As I look back on it, I can't believe that I remember some things as clear as day, even when I was five years old. We were living at the home place on what is now Evans Road in Nash County, just three and one-half miles from Nashville, the county seat. When I was a boy, it was a red, slippery clay road that led up a hill to Lawrence Evans' house and sawmill. I can still hear that Evans log truck straining to get up the hill, with Mr. Evans and his boys pushing and pulling from all sides. Just how long it would take them to get up the hill always generated amusing speculation.

My old house is now empty and in desperate need of repair, but it still stands like a soldier at attention, defiant, ready for action, and pleading for a tenant. We called it "the Home Place," a farm bought for ten thousand dollars from Margaret E. Deans on February 8, 1919, by my then-twenty-three-year-old daddy, Roy A. Cooper, and his brother, Dewey. Times were tough, and in 1924 Uncle Dewey sold his interest to Daddy. Although it was hard to make the ninety-eight-dollar semiannual payments on the twenty-eight-hundred-dollar mortgage to the Federal Land Bank of Columbia, Daddy finally paid off the loan in 1942. He always praised the Federal Land Bank for "being so lenient" with him. Looking back on it, I figure the bank knew no one would buy at foreclosure, or they were just happy Daddy always made his six percent interest payments on time.

I lived at the Home Place from 1927 to 1932, the first five years of my life. No electricity, no running water, no radio, no TV, no air-conditioning, no central heat—just a lot of love and memories.

Brownie

FOR INSTANCE, I'll never forget Brownie. Mother told me that cow's milk did not agree with me. "You can't keep down anything but goat's milk," she declared. So we bought a goat and named her "Brownie." When I called, "Brownie, Brownie, Brownie," she would come running. We had lots of adventures, and not always pleasant.

One day, my normally calm and stoic daddy stormed into the house in a rage. "Lois!" he exclaimed. "Do you know what that stupid goat has done? She tried to lie down on top of my truck cab!" In those days a 1928 pickup truck had a leather top. There wasn't much left of that truck top after Brownie ended up on the seat behind the steering wheel. "I'm gonna get rid of that goat. She's only a nuisance now." I started crying, of course. That was the only time I ever heard my mother yell at my father. "A nuisance? Well, look at your son. Is *he* a nuisance? Without Brownie, he wouldn't be here!" Needless to say, we never got rid of Brownie.

Dusty Dog

I HAD ANOTHER PET, a little dog named Chink. I have never known where in the world we got that name. Although my daddy owned and was paying off the mortgage on the land where we lived and farmed, he also rented a farm called the "Wrennie Place," located about one and one-half miles away. I remember Mother, Daddy, and I riding back and forth to the Wrennie Place with Chink running behind. He was always either dusty or muddy traveling the unpaved road, which was bumpy in dry weather and slushy in wet weather.

Fire in the Night

IN "BARNING TOBACCO" TIME, Daddy and Mother would have to stoke the tobacco barn furnace all night with wood to cure the tobacco. The curing process occurred when the tobacco was hung on sticks in a heated barn until it dried out and could be taken to market. Mother stayed up until midnight for her shift, and Daddy took the shift from then until daybreak. Since both of them had to be away from home, they carried me with them. My bed was a rough brown cotton sheet made of sewn-together fertilizer bags and spread on the corn in the corncrib, with Chink always snoozing at my side.

In those days curing tobacco meant seeing a column of smoke during the day and a red glow at night. This process was an out-of-control fire waiting to happen. Such a fire could occur when a stick of tobacco fell on a hot flue, or a spark from the furnace ignited a tobacco leaf. If that wasn't enough, the curing barns seemed to attract lightning. If a curing barn caught on fire and buckets of water did not stop the flames, the barn just burned down with all the tobacco in it and the poor farmer sadly looking on. Fire trucks were just for town.

Well, it happened to us at the Wrennie Place. Chink and I were in the corncrib fast asleep. The next thing I knew, Mother was standing over me, crying hysterically. Chink was barking, and the air was filled with smoke. I cracked the crib door open, but Mother wouldn't let me out. I saw Daddy standing with his head down, three or four men looking at him with sympathy. They had seen the fire and had come to help, but they were too late. Losing a barn of tobacco was a big hit financially to a farmer who was trying to make ends meet. The men knew and felt his loss.

Our Good Name

FOR MANY YEARS thereafter I heard my daddy say, "In 1932 I didn't make enough money to pay the interest on the Federal Land Bank mortgage on my farm. Bob Whitley lent me that money without a mortgage, note, or anything. Bob told me that my word was good enough, and he was right. I paid him back every penny." And to me he said, "Boy, your good name is worth more than money." My daddy was a smart man.

CHAPTER TWO

Forbidden Fruit

My first playmate was Allen Cooper. He and I lived about five hundred yards from each other on Evans Road. We were the same age, born in the same year 1927, and, by the time we were old enough to visit each other, our adventures, or should I say misadventures, began.

Allen's mother, Miss Rada, as all the children called her, was one of the sweetest mamas in the neighborhood, but on one occasion Allen and I tested her good nature. It was all the fault of red cherries hanging just out of reach on a tree located on the side of the road between his house and mine.

Well, it all happened this way. On a sunny spring morning, I got up rather early, ate breakfast, went out on the front porch, and happened to look down toward Allen's house. He was standing in the middle of the road. When he saw me, he waved his arm in the air, motioning me to come quickly. I immediately swung around and nearly bumped into my mother, who was standing in the doorway.

"Mother, may I…?" I began.

She smiled and finished my sentence for me. "… go to Allen's house? Yes, you may, but be a nice boy and don't worry Rada." We used the word "worry" as another word for "bother." Although we didn't know it yet, we were about to worry Rada a lot.

I jumped off the porch and started in a slow trot toward Allen, who was standing in the road waiting for me. As I drew near, I saw that he was staring pensively at the cherry tree on the side of the road. We had looked at that tree ever since it had bloomed, waiting impatiently for the little green cherries to appear. When they finally began to form, we waited week after week, watching them grow slowly into big green cherries that gradually changed to pink. Impatient as we were, our attention had been diverted, and the cherries faded from memory—until that moment. It was with astonishment that I realized where Allen was pointing and heard him yell, "Look at the cherries! They're ripe!"

I looked and sure enough, the cherries were blood red, hanging from the tree in clusters.

Even though we had just finished breakfast, our taste buds began screaming for those big, juicy cherries. We started running, but just as we got to the tree, we heard the rattle of a window going up, and Miss Rada's high-pitched voice warning, "You boys better remember what I told you. Climb that tree and I'm gonna whip both of you! You can have all the cherries you can reach standing on the ground, but no climbing up that tree. You hear me? It's too dangerous. You disobey me and I'll tan your hide!"

Allen and I meekly nodded and answered in unison, "Yes, ma'am."

We began to go around and around the tree. "Golly, look at all those cherries just hangin' there. But we can't reach any of 'em. What are we gonna do?" I wondered.

Allen started jumping with his arms reaching upward in an effort to grab a limb and bend it down so that we could reach the cherries before letting the limb go, but all his efforts proved fruitless.

"Heck! We can't get to 'em; the limbs are too high up," grumbled Allen, almost out of breath from jumping up, falling down, and just missing the high limbs.

"Hey! I got an idea," I ventured. "Maybe I can put my arms around you and hold you up so you can grab a limb and pull it to the ground."

"Good thinking," Allen agreed. He stood straight up and lifted his arms. I stooped down, bent my knees, wrapped my arms around his legs, and started lifting him up. That worked for about three inches, then *thud*. We both hit the hard ground. *Whoosh!* The breath rushed out of us. "Any more ideas?" Allen groaned.

"Well, maybe we can place something next to the tree high enough so that by standing on it and grabbing the tree trunk, we can reach that big limb and climb up in the tree. We can eat all the cherries we want!"

Hope springs eternal, and Allen quickly agreed to the new plan. Then we fell silent, thinking about whether or not we could get away with disobeying Miss Rada. The spell was broken when we heard a strange noise. We both looked quickly at the kitchen window, but Miss Rada was nowhere to be seen.

"It's just Spot," Allen laughed in relief. Allen's dog had whimpered, biting a flea that was interrupting his sleep.

"Where can we get something high enough to stand on?" I asked.

Allen thought a minute. "There's an old stone jar in the garage. It's empty and will be the very thing. It's pretty heavy, though."

"Let's get goin'," I eagerly responded.

"Hold it! Mama'll see us from the kitchen window if we're not careful."

We eyed each other nervously. Allen finally said, "OK. You lead. I'll follow."

"Why me? It's your house. We'll look more suspicious if I lead," I hedged.

The front of the house was only about fifty yards from us, but it seemed like a hundred. We moved slowly and stepped gingerly on our tiptoes, trying to walk quietly over the soft, newly plowed ground. We were terrified that Miss Rada would hear our footsteps. Actually you couldn't have heard a big mule walking on that soft ground, a fact that completely escaped us.

We finally reached the front of the house, safely out of the view of the kitchen window where Miss Rada spent much of her time preparing all kinds of good things to eat.

"OK. Let's plan our next move. We've got to be careful. The back door's the problem," Allen explained carefully. "Mama goes in and out that door a lot, and we got to go by there to get to the garage where the jar's just sittin' there waitin' for us." The back door led to a screened-in porch where Miss Rada put freshly baked cakes and pies to cool, and she could be counted on to go in and out of that door many times per day.

"Well, heck, if she happens to see us, we can just say we decided to play in the garage," Allen reassured himself and me. "Just don't act suspicious!" He looked around furtively and whispered, "All right. Who goes first? You or me?"

"Good grief, Allen. We go together. Didn't you just say we didn't want to look suspicious? Just act normal," I warned.

"OK. OK. Here we go again," Allen mumbled.

We started walking slowly on our way to the garage, and as we neared the pump house, which was just two or three yards from the back porch, I noticed that Allen was still tiptoeing. Gritting my teeth, I tapped his shoulder and pointed at his feet. He dropped off his tiptoes, his face flushing with embarrassment, and followed me.

I stopped, reached back, and pulled him beside me. "Remember, you said act normal!" I reminded him.

We continued our slow walk, past the porch, turning to give the back door an anxious look. Both of us held our breath and were just beginning to sigh with relief when Miss Rada suddenly came out of the kitchen door on to the back porch. We froze. She was carrying a steaming dish that she set on the back porch table. Seeing us, she asked, "You boys already eat enough cherries?"

Allen and I answered simultaneously. "Yes, ma'am," I said, as Allen answered, "No, ma'am." Noting the disparity, we both quickly changed our answers. "No, ma'am," I croaked at the same moment Allen blurted "Yes, ma'am." Allen and I looked at each other, and Miss Rada's eyes widened a bit with curiosity and maybe a little suspicion. We resumed our trek to the garage but with a noticeable increase in speed. We glanced back to see Miss Rada still standing on the porch looking at us, which may account for the fact that we just didn't notice that the garage door was half closed. You guessed it. We both stuck in the little opening. It took some flailing of arms and legs, but we finally struggled through.

When we were safely in the garage my first words were, "You reckon your mama suspects anything?"

"It's hard to fool Mama," Allen replied.

After a few minutes of weighing the gravity of the situation, our adventurous minds and rumbling stomachs decided that the risk was worth taking.

We got on each side of the stone jar and attempted to lift it, but to no avail. That was one heavy jar!

At last determination overcame the almost impossible. We turned the jar so that it would roll to the open door. When we reached the exit, we stopped, our smiles fading into grim frowns.

“What if Mama sees us? I know Mama; she’s smart. She’ll say, ‘What on earth are you children doing?’ What’re we gonna say?” Allen directed his question to me.

My answer: “I don’t know.”

We sat down on the jar to ponder our predicament. Can you imagine how little five-year-olds would approach this problem? I’ll bet our brain cells were working overtime. To this day I believe our final game plan was a good one. Maybe exercising those young brain cells was one of the reasons Allen and I were among the very few in our community to go on to college. But back to the story.

Allen reasoned, “When we go out that door we got three ways to go, but it looks like to me it’s best to go that way.” He pointed to the left. “There’s just a few feet from the garage door to the corner. She can’t see the other side of the garage from the porch. So we turn the corner, roll the jar down the far side of the garage, turn one more corner, and go down the back of the garage where Mama can’t see a thing. And then we can hide in the corn rows ’til we get to the tree! What’s wrong with that?” Allen’s expression now was one of sheer delight. Problem solved!

“Allen, you got it all figured out. I never would’ve thought of that,” I congratulated him. “The only problem I see is that we’re gonna get sheep burrs all over us in the corn rows. But that’s still the best way to go.” Sheep burrs are small, prickly little seed pods that hurt when they stick in you.

We quickly followed the game plan, sweat rolling into our eyes and chests heaving for breath. A push through the plowed ground brought us—Allen, the stone jar, and me—to the corn rows. The corn was planted on high ridges called rows, which were made by a turning plow. Between the rows was a flat surface called the “middle” that had been smoothed by a cotton plow with long blades. Tall corn with long, slender leaves drooped downward over the middle and made a perfect tunnel. The preparation of the rows and middles had been completed long enough so that the middles were hard, and made rolling the stone jar not too difficult for two determined five-year-old country boys. The only deterrent was the inevitable sheep burrs that grew in almost every cornfield. It seemed that if you passed within a foot of a sheep burr bush, the burrs would hop on you, stick to your clothes and wreak havoc with your skin. We wore overalls, which protected our chests and legs, but our thin cotton shirts were the perfect landing field for the burrs. Allen and I looked at each other and nodded, our signal to head for the tree. "We ain't got far," I encouraged.

Allen answered, "Let's get goin' then."

Rolling the jar was easy compared to pulling the burrs off our clothes. We had to stop every few yards to scratch our backs and arms. Finally with a muffled yell, I pointed to the cherry tree. "Quiet, don't be so loud. Mama'll hear us if we make too much noise," Allen cautioned.

We placed the jar behind the trunk of the tree, away from the prying kitchen window. "You first," I said.

Allen rubbed his hands together, stood on the jar, reached for a lower limb near the tree trunk, and scrambled up.

"I'm comin' up," I grunted. I reached for the same lower limb that Allen was on.

"Look at those cherries. Have you ever seen so many?" Allen said in a voice much too loud, I thought.

"There must be a bushel on this one limb, but we've got to go a little farther out on the limb to get 'em," I chimed in.

Allen and I started inching closer to the cherries when suddenly we heard Miss Rada. She was running toward us, apron flapping and eyes flashing, yelling, "You young'uns know what I said. Get out of that tree right now!"

We did. *Crack! Whoosh!* The limb we were sitting on broke at the tree trunk and hurtled down with Allen and me hanging on. The smaller, drooping branches growing down from the larger limb cushioned our fall.

We could hear Miss Rada screaming, "Lordy, Lordy, oh my Lord. Please don't let them be hurt."

As if to answer her, Allen, with a muffled sob, yelled, "We're all right, Mama."

"Oh, thank you, Lord," she breathed fervently and began to cry.

Allen and I were surprised. We had thought Miss Rada was going to yank us up by the collar and give us a good spanking.

A few minutes after the fall, however, her relief subsided and we knew that our first thought was right. A whipping was no longer on hold.

"First of all, you and Tommy are gonna pick every last cherry off that limb. If I come out here again and find one cherry on this broken limb, you will get *two* whippin's. Now both of you come with me to the kitchen for a dishpan and a bucket," Miss Rada commanded. "If you fill them up, come back in here and empty them and go back until all of those cherries on that limb are here in this kitchen."

We hung our little heads, took the pan and bucket, and slowly walked back to begin our job.

When we got to the tree, we stopped. "Did that little limb grow some since we left?" Allen whined.

"And can you believe all those cherries hangin' on all those little limbs that're sproutin' out from the big limb?" I added.

"Well, we better start pickin'. You know what Mama said," Allen uttered gloomily.

We picked cherries, and we picked and picked, too intent on filling the containers and too sick with worry to eat a single one.

After at least an hour, we stopped and sat down to rest in the shade of the tree. Allen turned to me and said, "All our planning, all our work, and what'd we git? A whippin', that's what. Mama's gonna whip me, and she's gonna tell your mother, and she's gonna whip you."

We both began to cry tears of frustration and regret. "I told you we ought not to do it," I sobbed.

"You did not!" Allen wailed.

"Well, we talked about whether we should do it. You know we knowed it was wrong. We both tried to keep Miss Rada from catchin' on to what we wuz doin'."

"You did *not* say we ought not to do it! You *know* you didn't." Allen's voice seemed to rise with each word, getting louder and louder, his dirt-streaked face turning pink, then red.

"Well, anyway, I *thought* it," I yelled back.

"*Thought it* ain't the same as *sayin' it*!" Allen retorted.

"You thought it too, and it *is* the same thing. You and me both thought it was wrong."

"Well, I reckon you're right," Allen reluctantly agreed. "We both knowed it was wrong."

We were little crooks who had been caught, and we knew we were guilty. To keep the punishment from being worse, we remorsefully returned to our job and finally finished picking every last cherry off that broken limb. We carried them to the kitchen to find Miss Rada busily preparing dinner, back then the midday meal. Supper was the evening meal. When she saw that we had nearly filled the bucket and pan full of cherries, she looked surprised. "My goodness! Look at all those cherries! Well, you boys at least worked hard," she said with a slight smile. "Tommy, you go home. You've been here since seven o'clock this morning, and it's almost ten-thirty. Lois'll be worried."

I immediately started up the road to my house. I walked very slowly, thinking to myself, "*Lois* will be worried. She won't be half as worried as I am. I know Miss Rada's gonna tell Mother and Mother's gonna whip me."

When I finally got home, Mother was in the kitchen preparing dinner. She turned when I came in and asked, "Did you have a good time? You must have. You were gone a long time."

"Yes, ma'am," I answered.

"What did you and Allen do all morning? Pick cherries?"

"We sure did!" I answered fervently.

I was miserable. I knew that Miss Rada was going to tell Mother what we had done and I was in for a whipping. I wandered around the house until I got tired of that, wandered out in the yard, and glumly walked all the way around the house. On the second trip I saw Allen in the road coming toward me. "This is it. He's coming to tell Mother," I sobbed. The tears flooded my eyes so that I could hardly see as I ran toward Allen. "Miss Rada sent you to tell Mother about this morning, didn't she? Did she whip you?" I asked between sobs.

"No, no! No, she didn't whip me, and no, she only said to ask your mother to let you come back to my house to have some hot cherry pie before it gets cold." Allen grinned happily at me, relief brightening his face.

I was so astounded by the turn of events that my first thought was that Allen was playing a dreadful trick on me. "Allen, if you're tellin' a story, I'm gonna get you good," I shouted hysterically.

"I'm tellin' you the truth," Allen protested. "Mama said she was so relieved that we didn't get hurt. I told her how we talked about how it was wrong and we ought not to have done it. I reckon that was the reason she decided not to whip me and not to tell your mama."

I was so happy I jumped on the porch and ran in the house

yelling, “Mother, Mother, Miss Rada invited me to her house to have some hot cherry pie.”

Mother looked surprised. “You just came from Rada’s house. You were there all morning.”

“Please, Mother. Allen’s outside waitin’,” I begged.

“Well, for goodness sakes. Go ahead. Rada must be a glutton for punishment having you boys the whole morning.”

I ran out of the door. My joy and relief chased away all my sadness, and we started happily down the road back to Miss Rada’s house.

You know to this day—I’m now eighty years old—I still think of the cherry tree when I pass that house and the lesson Miss Rada taught Allen and me and did it without the whipping we probably deserved.

WILLIE ED JR. was one of our playmates, and he was coming off Miss Rada’s back porch one day, eating a biscuit and preserves. He was asked by his father, who was passing through the yard going back to the fields to work, “Boy, who gave you that ’serves and biscuit?” The answer was memorable. “That old, sweet, fat Miss Rada Cooper!”

He tried to get it right. We all knew what he meant. As for me, on the day of the cherry tree, if I had been asked the same question, I would have said, “That young, slender, mighty sweet Miss Rada Cooper.”

Miss Rada and her husband, Uncle Cray, had four children: three girls, Teency, Dot, and Faye, and one son, Allen. All of her children did well. They grew up to be good citizens and good people.

Allen and I were friends for life. We got baptized in Elm Grove Baptist Church together, went through grade school, Oak Ridge Academy, a short stint in the navy, graduated from Wake Forest, courted together, and married hometown girls. I later graduated from the University of North Carolina at Chapel Hill School of Law and came back to practice law in Nashville. Allen became a successful businessman and farmer in Nashville and Rocky Mount. Our professions took us in different directions, and we didn't see each other as much as I would have liked. I regret that, since we had a lot in common.

Allen was born April 4, 1927, twenty-two days after my birthday. I was always teasing him that I was older and that he would have to listen to me and take my advice. Allen died on September 8, 1997. He was a good friend. I miss him.

CHAPTER THREE

There's No Place Like Home

Leaving Home

THE COBB PLACE, as we called it, was located about three miles west of Nashville, off Highway 64. I'll never forget my grief at leaving my home and my friends and traveling the six long miles to live at this farm. My parents figured the only way to make ends meet was to farm out the Home Place on "half shares" with a tenant and rent the Cobb Place to farm ourselves.

At first I was excited about the move, but then I realized I would be leaving Allen, Dewey Lee, Brother, and the rest of my playmates. Six miles was a long way in those days, and five years old was mighty young to pull up roots, but it had to be done. We moved in the latter part of 1933 just in time to start the new crop for the coming year.

The house and farm together were called the Cobb Place. Our two-story house, said to be haunted, was located off the highway about two miles down a dirt path, up on a hill. The outbuildings consisted of a three-room house, tobacco barns, and corncribs.

I never did find out what was supposed to be haunting the Cobb house, but I was more than a little apprehensive and fascinated exploring dark corners in large rooms and creeping up the winding stairway to the one huge room at the top of the stairs. Downstairs in the sitting room fireplace we had to use "barn" wood for fires. Daddy would haul in the four-foot logs usually used to cure tobacco and light them for warmth and sometimes for cooking in the cavernous chimney. The resulting fire was cozy and helped me grow accustomed to my new home.

Although I missed my playmates, I quickly accepted my role as an only child. Actually I was always pretty much of a loner anyway. I did not mind being by myself, but I really did miss my dog, Chink. He died, I suppose, of old age, or maybe he couldn't take the move, but he was a part of me I did not want to give up. Daddy must have understood my sorrow. Not long after we moved, he drove up one day with not one puppy, but two. I was ecstatic. We named the boy Rock and the girl Julie. They were one-year-old beagle hounds—rabbit dogs—but Daddy never had time to hunt, so they became full-time pets and my companions.

Kelly

I HAD ANOTHER COMPANION, Kelly Yarborough, who had come to work for us about three months before we left home. He helped me avert some of the loneliness. His parents and brothers and sisters lived where Nead Evans's house is now located, at the intersection of Old Bailey Highway and Rose Loop Road. After he had worked for us about two weeks back home, his father, learning that we were moving to the Cobb Place, told Daddy that Kelly could go with us to help work on the farm. Kelly quickly agreed because he got paid working for us and didn't get paid working at home. Also I knew he liked us, and we really liked him, too. Kelly was coal black with beautiful white teeth, about six feet tall, muscular, and handsome. I remember now with fondness Kelly saying, "Gimme some ham," and he would then grab me in the back of the leg where it really tickled. He'd laugh his loud and merry laugh. I can hear him now.

In the summer of 1932, the weather was unusually hot. Daddy and Kelly were constantly plowing cotton and tobacco, leaving little time for Kelly to pal around with me. My job was to keep the two men supplied with water, and it seemed to me that just as I was starting to inspect a "doodle bug" hole or carefully bend a thorny rosebush limb to peer into a new bird nest, Mother would be at the well drawing a fresh bucket of water and filling two quart jars. I knew before she even called that it was time for me to transport the water to Daddy and Kelly in the field.

I don't remember how many acres of cropland had been cleared at the Cobb Place, but there was one huge field surrounded by woods, and there was a small path running around the edge of the woods. The path was only wide enough for a mule and tobacco truck, which was a small rectangular wooden slide pulled by a mule. The path was sandy in some spots and in some places overgrown by dog fennels, a shoulder-high green bunchy weed. Farther along and over the path you could find briars, sometimes fragrant with white blooms entwined in honeysuckle vines and sometimes to my delight filled with big, juicy, sweet blackberries hanging in clusters bowing over the path, seeking sunlight. Oh, were they tasty! If you ventured off the path, there were always mysteries to explore: birds' nests, hollow trees, squirrels jumping from tree to tree, rocks to throw at the squirrels, and hollow logs where I kept hoping to find a possum.

I can still hear Daddy's irritated voice. "Tommy, where in the world have you been? You've been gone over an hour." How was a six-year-old supposed to answer a question like that? I explained weakly, "I just been coming down the path. It's a long way."

I would bring the water, one quart jar under one arm and one quart jar under the other. Sometimes when I hurried from my secret adventures I would drop a jar in the plowed ground and sometimes I would arrive with just one jar; the other would lie broken somewhere along the journey from the house to my destination. When this happened, Daddy would be disgusted, and I can now see why. Both he and Kelly would be drenched with sweat, their shirts clinging to their bodies, their pants completely soaked, and where their pants legs stopped at their shoes there would be wet soil sticking to the shoes and to the bottoms of the pants legs.

On one of these occasions, Daddy said, "Kelly, I don't have any kind of 'catching' disease; do you?"

Kelly answered, "Not that I know of, Mr. Roy."

Daddy turned to me and said, not unkindly, "Tell Lois to fill just one half-gallon jar. Kelly and I will both drink from the same jar." After that, with one arm free, even though I sometimes lingered a little too long on the path, I did do a better job of arriving with a fresh jar of water.

Puttin' in Tobacco

THE CROPS GREW FAST that summer, or that's the way it seemed to me; the tobacco harvesting, or "puttin' in" tobacco as we called it, started early. I was too young to be of much help. Even though I begged him, Daddy wouldn't let me truck. Hauling the tobacco from the fields in a narrow wooden slide pulled by a mule was dangerous. Daddy was afraid the heavy truck filled with green tobacco would overturn on me. That happened sometimes even with an adult trucking. That first harvest at the Cobb Place was certainly easier on

Mother, because Kelly took Mother's place tending to the barn the first part of the night curing the tobacco. She didn't have to do it like she did at the Home Place.

Daddy would let me go with him to Nashville to get the "hands" or the "help." Both words were used to describe workers in those days. On the first day of the tobacco harvest, Mother came to the bedroom where I slept all by myself at the Cobb house and asked, "Do you really want to get up this early and go with your Daddy to get the hands?"

I was excited. I answered her by jumping out of bed, grabbing my overalls, sticking in one leg, hopping around to put the other leg in, pulling up my pants, and running to the kitchen in my unlaced shoes. Daddy was just finishing his last cup of coffee. He slid his chair back, looked at the old alarm clock on the ancient pie safe, and said, "Well, it's five o'clock. By the time I get there and back, it'll be time to start." He walked over to get his hat.

Thrusting a ham biscuit in my hand as I rushed by her, Mother admonished, "Tommy, you haven't had a thing to eat. You can eat breakfast when you get back," she yelled, but I was already following Daddy to the truck.

When I got to the 1928 Ford truck, which was black like all Fords in those days, the motor was already running, and the usual smoke was pouring out of the exhaust pipe. I climbed in and slammed the door twice. Daddy reached over and slammed it shut a third time with a mighty bang, and we were off.

Those days the help was mostly from a section of town called Brooklyn where one person, usually a woman, had previously arranged with Daddy to hire the help. We would drive up in our pickup, and the "help" would come running out and jump in the back of the truck. Sometimes one who had promised to come would not show up. Clara, the woman we had hired to assemble the workforce, would yell, "Sam!" or "Junior!" or some other name, and the missing "hand" would come running. Sometimes too many would show up, and they would fuss and argue as to who got to go; both work and money were scarce in those days. Of course, Clara would settle the argument, and off we would go.

Mother's Unexpected Guest

BEFORE I KNEW IT, tobacco barning time came and went. The cotton leaves were beginning to turn red, and I could detect a white spot here and there, the cotton bolls peeking out one by one. Poplar leaves were green, yellow, and red, a rainbow on each tree. August gusts, ushering in the rainy season, were over, and the sky was a deep blue. I remember clear and chilly September mornings.

It was just such a morning that Daddy came in the kitchen with what seemed to me a puzzled, worried look. "Lois," he said, "you know what? There's a man in the corncrib. I've never seen him before, and I know he's not from around here. Why, we're a mile from the highway. I tell you, it makes me uncomfortable."

If Daddy was uncomfortable, I was frightened, but Mother said, "Why don't you go invite him in to breakfast?" I was astounded. Daddy was skeptical, but he didn't say anything as he went out to issue the invitation. In a few minutes he came back with a white man who looked about thirty-five or forty years old. He had on pants that had holes in each knee, a blue work shirt with one sleeve torn off at the elbow. His hair was hanging down his back, a phenomenon unseen in that day and time.

Mother ventured a question. "Where're you from?"

He answered, "Up the road."

Mother tried again. "Up the road?"

He answered, "A long way from here."

"How long have you been walkin'?"

"A long time," he mumbled between bites.

Mother finally gave up. She satisfied herself instead with piling on the biscuits, eggs, and ham. She knew she was getting nowhere.

The visitor finally finished his breakfast, pushed back his chair, stood up, and said, "Ma'am, that was the best breakfast I ever had. You're a nice lady." And he left. We never saw him again.

That's just the way Mother was.

The Perils of Grading Tobacco

THE SEASONS PASSED QUICKLY after that. There was cotton picking time, and we again rounded up the "hands" in Nashville. After cotton picking time came and went, grading tobacco time was upon us when we carefully separated the cured tobacco leaves into first grade, called "wrappers," for cigars; second grade, called red tobacco, cured too much; green tobacco, primed before it was ripe; and trash. The cured tobacco had to be graded before we took it to the market. We had a special "grading room," a little house that was surrounded by high weeds and grass, and our income depended on the quality of our tobacco. Today tobacco is thrown together and bailed. Sort of takes the challenge out of it.

But in those days, after the tobacco was graded, it was tied in bundles by using a tobacco leaf to bind the stems. The bundles were then hung on a "grading" stick, which was really a tobacco stick that was trimmed until it was smooth so that it would not tear the tobacco leaves. The next step was to press the tobacco by standing on a board placed over the stick. Next the tobacco was piled on the floor ready to be hauled to the market. It was not unusual for this process to take place at night.

On one of those nights, Mother was walking to the grading room carrying a lantern. Daddy was following her with an arm full of grading sticks, and I was close behind. I gasped with fear when Daddy suddenly yelled, "Lois, watch out! There's a highland moccasin right at the door!" Mother stumbled up the steps, dropping the lantern, leaving all of us in complete blackness.

Daddy shouted, "Lois, stay in the grading room; Tommy, you run back up the path!"

Next I heard a loud crack. Daddy had thrown the sticks on the ground and jumped up and down on them. As soon as Mother got the lantern lit again, Daddy slowly picked up the sticks one by one, and sure enough on the bottom of the pile there lay a strikingly patterned thirty-inch snake, with a shiny copper-colored head squashed by Daddy's dance on the sticks. Daddy was right to be careful. The highland moccasin—or copperhead, as that kind of snake is called—has a venomous bite. It was another episode in my young life that I'll never forget.

Rock and Julie

IN FACT, life at the Cobb Place was full of unforgettable episodes, not the least of which was the story of my dogs, Rock and Julie.

One fall morning I was awakened by Julie, howling painfully. I went out on the porch and found her walking up and down, whimpering and yelping. I ran into the kitchen and found Daddy sitting at the table waiting for breakfast while Mother was cooking the usual ham and eggs.

I said, "Daddy! Something's wrong with Julie. She's howling like she's hurt."

Mother spoke gently. "Honey, she's been doing that all night."

"She must be hurt," I said. "We ought to take a look at her."

Daddy stopped me. "Slow down, son. I've already looked at her, and I can't find any injury or anything wrong with her."

After breakfast Daddy and I went on the porch to find Julie still pacing up and down, and, as we approached, she began what I would describe as a whimper. She almost made me cry. I said, "Daddy, she looks so sad." I took her in my arms to comfort her, but it was not to be. She looked at me with mournful eyes and emitted that sad little whimper.

Suddenly Daddy asked, "Where's Rock? I haven't seen him all morning. He's probably off running a rabbit, but that's strange. Julie would certainly be with him. Maybe that's why she's so upset." Julie and Rock were beagle hounds, and even though Daddy was too busy and no one else was around to rabbit hunt, Julie and Rock would run rabbits together. We would often hear them in the woods and fields doing what they were bred to do, chase rabbits.

It hadn't occurred to me that Rock was missing because I'd been so concerned with Julie. To tell you the truth, I loved both of those dogs. Rock was a little more playful than Julie, but they would both roll with me on the ground under the barn shelter or anywhere else I, or should I say we, decided to play. Rock was bigger than Julie. He had long legs and Julie had short legs. I remember, too, that Julie would always stop playing before Rock. No doubt about it, Julie was the more intelligent. When the two of them were hunting, Julie would give out a little yelp and Rock would come running, for he knew that Julie had picked up the scent of a rabbit. They were always together, like Siamese twins.

All through the next day, Julie continued her traumatic howling and whimpering, and to my dismay she refused to eat. Daddy came up to me on the third day and said, "You know, I think something's happened to Rock. He's never stayed away from home this long before."

We never saw Rock again, and a few days after that, Julie was gone. We searched and searched to no avail. A week or two later, Daddy found her body lying out in a broom straw field. Mother and Daddy both agreed that Julie had grieved herself to death.

It was a sad time for all of us, especially for a six-year-old, suffering through another loss. Chink had died the year before.

First Grade in Nashville

BUT LIFE GOES ON, and at last it was September, and boy, was I excited. It was a new adventure for me, one that I had looked forward to for a long time. I was going to school! Daddy and Mother had talked to me (I think from the day I was born) about the importance of school—Daddy especially. He actually led me to believe that school was the most important thing in my young life and that if I dropped out of school, "You'll amount to nothing." Mother took a different tack; she was always telling me to behave. "Don't get in with the wrong crowd, and always pay attention to your teacher."

Well, finally the first day of school arrived. I was up early and ran into the kitchen to find Mother packing my newly purchased lunchbox with sandwiches, peanut butter and crackers, and an apple. Daddy was sitting at the table sipping coffee, waiting for Mother to fix breakfast. Nonchalantly he remarked, "Lois, you're fixin' enough food for the whole first grade." He was trying to be casual, but I could see it in his eyes; he was as excited as I was. Later during breakfast I could see that Mother was too. Both Mother and Daddy were talking at the same time, telling me what to do and what not to do. I enjoyed the attention.

After breakfast Daddy and Mother walked with me out on the porch to see me off. I was dressed in my new apron overalls and brogan shoes. I would walk about one and one-half miles to meet the school bus on old Highway 64. I knew well the route to the school bus stop. It led through a field into the woods and out again to the Askew

Batchelor place where Russell Batchelor lived. I had traveled it many times to visit Russell and to play with Trixie, his devoted German shepherd. Trixie accepted me, although she would go through the screen door after Russell's mother if she tried to paddle him. Russell was about two years older than I was, and much later we would attend Wake Forest College together, where he would become a star baseball player. Many times we met and finished the bus stop route together.

Before I had gotten twenty feet that first September morning, Mother yelled, "Wait! Wait! You forgot your lunch box." She went back in the house and quickly returned, bringing my forgotten lunch. She grabbed me and hugged and kissed me, turning her head and hurrying back up the steps, but not before I saw a stream of tears running down her cheeks. As I began my first journey to the school bus stop, I looked back several times. Mother waved at me. Daddy stood stoically with arms folded, but I knew he too probably wanted to cry. Grown men just didn't cry. I have only recently accepted that it is OK for men to cry.

My first year in school was in the old school building in Nashville, and my first-grade teacher was Mrs. White, a maternal lady with white hair. The very first day she began to teach about wildflowers, and I can remember only one thing. She told us about goldenrods and wanted someone to bring one to school the next day. Surprisingly, no one in the class except me, the country boy, knew what a goldenrod was. I could not wait. There was a whole field of them right behind my house, and the next day I was the only one who brought a goldenrod to school. Mrs. White made me feel like a knight in golden armor.

Meeting the School Bus: Never Say Never

ALTHOUGH I LOVED Mrs. White, sometimes I wanted to stay home from school like most children do. Early one morning I hustled out of my warm bed and ran to the big fireplace where a hot fire was crackling and sparks were leaping out between the four-foot logs. As usual it was cold in the big Cobb house, which made the fireplace especially inviting. Daddy was sitting in a corner next to the fire, not at his usual place at the kitchen table, waiting for Mother to serve the morning meal. I noticed he seemed a little worried. "What's the trouble, Daddy?" I asked.

He answered, "Well, it snowed last night. There's a big snow on the ground. I bet it's at least four inches."

I jumped up and down and yelled gleefully, "What's wrong with that?"

He retorted, "Well, I don't know how I'll get you to the school bus stop. I know that school won't be closed because I hear traffic on the highway, and the scrapers have cleared the road. But my old truck will never make it down the path."

"Well, then, I can just stay at home today," I beamed.

"No, you can't. You're going to school somehow."

Mother came in about that time. "Roy, you'll just have to carry him on your back."

Kelly had just come in the kitchen, bringing in an arm full of wood for the kitchen stove and overheard the conversation. He stuck his head in the door and said, "Miss Lois, I can take him on the mule."

Well, that was that. The next thing I knew I was dressed and out the door. Kelly was waiting for me in the edge of the yard. He had already bridled Old Mary, who was busy scratching the snow in search of grass. There was no saddle, therefore no stirrups to put my foot in to climb on her back. That did not pose a problem for Kelly. He grabbed me, hoisted me up on Mary's back, climbed up behind me, and we were off. I was grumbling because I did *not* want to go sit in a schoolroom when I could play all day long in the snow. Kelly reminded me, "You're a lucky boy to have parents that want you to go to school and make something of yourself."

As we neared the bus stop, I said, "Kelly, let me down."

"Why?"

"I don't want everybody laughing at me."

"If they laugh, it's just because they wish they could ride a mule to meet the school bus."

But after my furious protests, he let me down and I trudged on toward the bus stop, sloshing through the snow.

The last thing I heard from Kelly was, "You gonna get your feet wet. You just see." Well, he was right.

Friendship Survives Time

HOW WAS I TO KNOW, and I doubt that Kelly knew, that this mule ride in the snow to the school bus stop and our life at the Cobb Place would always be remembered by both of us and that our friendship would last until we passed from this earth? I know, because he stayed in touch with me. Much later, in 1945, he wrote me from his army post while I was at Wake Forest College. I answered, telling him about college life. After we stopped corresponding, I thought I would never hear from him again, but in 1959 (we were living on Cross Street in Nashville), I heard a knock at the door. I opened it, and to my surprise there stood Kelly. He was dressed to the nines in a black overcoat, a dark suit, and a black derby hat cocked to one side. He let out a big laugh, showing those beautiful white teeth, and yelled out, "Gimme some ham!" His hair was white, but at about fifty-five years he was still muscular and as handsome as ever. He told me he was married and working at the shipyard in Norfolk, Virginia. "When I came in to Nashville," he recounted, "I asked a man on the street, 'Where does Tommy Cooper live?' 'You mean Lawyer Cooper?' he asked me. 'I ain't looking for no lawyer,' I said. 'Well, I don't know any other Tommy Cooper,' he told me. So here I am. How about that. You're a big shot lawyer!" he grinned.

"Kelly," I responded, "you know I'm no big shot, just a country lawyer."

"That's the best kind!" he exclaimed.

We reminisced about our life at the Cobb Place and laughed about the mule ride in the snow. I'm sorry that I never saw or heard from him again. I don't know if or when Kelly died, but how he lived and what he meant to me will always be fresh in my memory.

Vanilla

MY YEAR AT the Cobb Place was about to end. The tenant at the Home Place was not farming to suit Daddy, so he and Mother decided to move once more. That meant that I was to leave Nashville School and enter second grade at Deans, a two-room school located near the Home Place. Daddy was upset about that for he knew (and he was right) that Nashville School was much better for me. In the years of the Depression, however, some tough choices had to be made. I was happy because I would be with my old playmates, but I was a little sad to leave my many new friends at Nashville.

One day, just before school was out for the summer (Daddy would not move until I had finished the school year), Daddy picked me up from school in his old truck. When I opened the door to get in, I saw a tiny nose sticking out of his coat pocket. As I looked closer, a little head popped out. Daddy smiled, ran his hand down in his pocket, and pulled out a tiny white puppy. "She's yours," he said.

I was dumbfounded. This was the cutest puppy I had ever seen. I blurted out, "Where did you get her?"

"Charlie Ward," he said, "and this puppy's name is Vanilla."

"Why Vanilla?"

"Well, Charlie said it seems like every time he sees you, you've got a cone of vanilla ice cream in your hand. He also said his little daughter Lillian talks about you all the time, and she wanted you to have the puppy."

That was news to me, but I was mighty happy about the puppy. Later in high school I did date Lillian Ward until I noticed a little seventh-grade girl with long black hair. Her name was Beverly, and Lillian was no match for her. No contest.

Home Again

IN ANY CASE, Vanilla became my friend and eased the transition from the Cobb Place back to the Home Place. Daddy was already setting out tobacco there, and as soon as the school year ended we made the transition, not back to the house on Evans Road, but to the little four-room house, up the hill ditches from the Old Bailey Highway where we would live for the rest of my young country life. Both houses were located on the farm called the Home Place.

Before the meager household furnishings were unloaded, Allen, Brother, Dewey Lee, and Thurston came walking up. The neighborhood grapevine had spread the news of our return. Everyone helped unload the truck. Then Daddy called to Mother, who was inside busily arranging her new home, "Lois, I'm going to get some help to move the stove." That was the only furniture we owned that needed more than two people to move it.

Allen, Dewey Lee, Brother, Thurston, and I jumped in the back of the truck to catch a ride as far as Uncle Dewey's house. I was home again!

Six miles doesn't seem like much to today's mobile society, but to this six-year-old country boy, who had never been to Washington or the beach or even Raleigh, it was huge. My year at the Cobb Place, six miles away from my boyhood friends, was potential disaster. Instead, this time enriched my life. From Mother and her homeless breakfast guest I learned the meaning of hospitality. From Daddy I learned the importance of a good education even before I started first grade. Kelly showed me that among friends skin color really doesn't matter. And, of course, I guess the most important lesson, in the end, was "There's no place like home."

My Nashville first grade classmates
(I'm second from the right on the second row.)

CHAPTER FOUR

The Honey Tree

MY GRANDFATHER ON Daddy's side, Pa Fed (James Pharoah Cooper), and my grandmother, Mama Lucy (Lucy J. Baines Cooper), lived less than a half-mile from my house on a narrow little dirt road, now Old Bailey Highway, State Road 1001. Even when I was only seven years old I would walk to their house. On these walks Mother and Daddy never worried about my safety, for the danger of being hit by a car in those days was unheard of. A car hardly ever passed and, if it did, it rarely exceeded thirty-five miles an hour.

On this particular day I jumped out of bed, ran to the kitchen, and gobbled down my breakfast of scrambled eggs, sausage, good hot biscuits and red-eyed gravy, and yelled, "Good-bye!" I vaguely heard my daddy ask, "Where's he going in such an all-fired hurry?" My mother sighed, "To your father's house or Dewey's where he'll probably meet Dewey Lee and Brother and the other children." And she was right.

Uncle Dewey, Daddy's brother, lived on Pa Fed's farm in a house that was only a stone's throw from Pa Fed's house. Uncle Dewey had seven children, quite a contrast to my home situation. This was usually the meeting place where I would rendezvous with Dewey Lee and Brother, whose real name was James McLain Cooper. Everyone called him "Brother"; I guess it was because his brothers and sisters called him that.

I jumped off the porch, surprising and frightening the chickens. They were scratching around in the front yard, and my sudden jump caused them to fly in every direction, screeching their protests as I headed toward the Old Bailey Highway down the flower-covered hill ditches that protected the path from erosion. Since my house was at the end of the path, I ran past the homes of Mr. Van, Uncle Bob, Uncle Brad, and Aunt Pat. I stopped occasionally to avoid a bumblebee or dig my heels in the two-track ruts made by mules and wagons and old pickup trucks used by the neighbors who lived on the path. And of course the fertilizer truck that came by in the spring along with an occasional visitor added to the depth of the ruts. On my walks, like everybody else, I avoided the blossoms gracing the mounds between the ruts and dragged my brogans in the sandy wheel tracts.

I was nearly out of breath when I reached Uncle Dewey's house. Dewey Lee was standing in the yard. "Are we really gonna cut down the honey tree this morning?" I asked.

Looking woeful, Dewey Lee responded, "No, Daddy couldn't find anybody to help him pull the crosscut saw."

My feathers flopped. But then I saw that mischievous grin on Dewey Lee's face, and I knew it was going to happen. That honey tree was coming down!

Finally Uncle Dewey, Brother, and Hoyt Williams came out on the front porch. "Brother, you get the saw; Dewey Lee, you get the ax; and, Tommy, you get the briar blade. Hoyt and I'll get dressed for the job," instructed Uncle Dewey. By getting dressed he meant putting on two pairs of pants, two shirts, and high-top shoes and then tying his pants legs. In those days no one had ever heard of a bee suit, and certainly not a "smoker," which later was used to scatter the bees and counter the bee stings.

In our community there were no beehives. As a matter of fact I had never heard of a beehive. Can you believe that only six years later I would be in the honey business with more than ten hives? But that's another story.

Uncle Dewey finished tying his pants legs, looked around, and called out, "Everybody ready? Then let's go."

The honey tree was located in the edge of the woods that led to the Cherry Hole, a small body of water that was a favorite place for us to swim, fish, and camp. No one knows why it was called the Cherry Hole, and no one knows how it was formed. It was located a few feet from the run of Sapony Creek but was never considered a part of the creek. It was simply the Cherry Hole, surrounded by big, tall pine trees of two species, loblolly and long straw. As the pine trees grew up toward the sky, the tree tops formed a canopy that prevented the sun from reaching the ground, which in turn kept other trees and underbrush from growing, creating a thick rug of pine needles. The sunrays, however, did invade a few spots in the treetops, the warmth permitting the tough little dogwoods to grow, their blooms adding to the beauty of the woods. To me, it was a big chapel... the sweet smell of dogwoods, complete quiet and peace.

At the edge of the field, the sun won the battle. There were a few gum trees, a few oaks, wildflowers, and honeysuckle, all protected by thick, thorny bushes, underbrush, and briars. Guess where the honey tree was! You guessed it. In the middle of the underbrush and briars!

Dewey Lee marveled, "Well, there she is. See that old dead oak? Boy, I'll bet that tree's a thousand years old!"

Uncle Dewey smiled. "Well, I don't think it's quite *that* old. But it's old."

I looked up. "Where're the bees?"

"Look at the lower limb," Brother chimed in. "The end is broken off, leaving a hollow. See the bees going in and out?"

"Oh, I see. The bees are really working." I kept my voice low and calm, trying to hide my excitement. "Are we gonna cut down the whole tree?"

"No," Brother smiled at my ignorance. "We'll just saw off the hollow limb with the bees and honey in it."

The hollow limb was about five feet up and much too high to be sawed off from the ground. Fortunately, Uncle Dewey had foreseen the problem and had already placed short ladders on each side of the tree trunk. Uncle Dewey and Hoyt were ready to ascend the ladders, Hoyt on one side and Uncle Dewey on the other. "All right, when this limb hits the ground, the bees will be mad as all fire, so you kids better get away from here as fast as you can," exclaimed Uncle Dewey.

Dewey Lee, Brother, and I followed this advice to a certain extent. We were adventurous and curious. We wanted to see the limb fall, so we went about four or five feet from the tree.

Uncle Dewey and Hoyt began sawing, and finally the limb, the home of the bees, hit the ground with a thud. Uncle Dewey and Hoyt dropped the saw and fled the scene. We "young'uns," as we were often called, being brave, not afraid of danger, and completely ignorant of the true state of events, calmly turned and began to walk slowly away. We had gone only about three steps when the angry bees began to fill the air around us. Brother and Dewey Lee ran toward the Cherry Hole away from danger. I had no sooner turned to follow when a bee found its target, its hot knife stinger stabbing over my right eye. Bees began buzzing in my hair. I panicked. I knew I had to escape the bees so I headed for the edge of the woods toward the field. The journey took me through briars, low-hanging limbs, and thorny bushes that tore at my clothes and skin, mercifully brushing away the bees. Finally I broke through to the open field. My right eye had swollen shut; my face and arms were bloody; my grown-up bravery was gone. I was a sobbing seven-year-old again.

I stumbled to Uncle Dewey's house. Aunt Lillian was in the yard. "My Lord, child, I looked out the window and saw you coming. I knew it! I knew it! I knew it! I knew somebody was gonna get stung. Come in the house right now."

"Take off all your clothes except your underwear," Aunt Lillian instructed firmly. While I was tearing at my overalls, she opened the pie safe, which held not only the pies when they were cooling, but also other household goods, including home medicines. First she smeared my forehead with an Arm & Hammer baking soda paste and followed that with a Railroad Snuff paste to my swollen eye, both remedies concocted by adding a little water to the soda and snuff. Immediate relief! Or so I thought. I lay down on the sofa and let her gentle loving care dry my tears. In about thirty minutes I felt well enough to go home.

My mother, like an old setting hen with her one chick, repeated the snuff and soda process begun by Aunt Lillian. By this time I was feeling much better.

Late that same afternoon, Dewey Lee came walking up the path. Mother, Daddy, and I were sitting on the front porch. Before he got in the yard, I yelled, "What're you doing here? Did they get the honey?"

"Two dishpans full, and everybody wants you to come and eat supper with us and spend the night," grinned Dewey Lee.

I spun around and blurted out, "Can I? Can I, Mother?"

Mother looked at Daddy, and his expression showed no objection. "Well," Mother said, "it looks to me like Lillian and Dewey would be tired of you spending the night so much, but I guess this is a special occasion, so go ahead."

I jumped off the porch, and Dewey Lee and I started for his house. It was almost dark when we arrived, and Uncle Dewey, Hoyt, and Brother were sitting on the front porch. In those days with no air conditioning it was too hot to be in the house before the sun went down unless, of course, you were in charge of preparing supper (nobody ever heard of "dinner" at night). The women and the girls had the hot job of preparing the meal no matter what the weather. I left Dewey Lee and the others on the porch and went back to the kitchen to tell Aunt Lillian that I was there and was going to spend the night. The old wood stove was throwing off a blanket of heat that caused the sweat to dampen my shirt and burn my eyes, but the smell of middling meat frying in the pan made me tarry. Nothing could beat the smell of that sizzling streak of lean streak of fat except perhaps the aroma of buttermilk biscuits baking in the oven. I stopped just long enough to hear Aunt Lillian say, "Glad you could come. Now we have the whole gang of honey hunters."

As I started back to the porch, I heard everybody laughing. Uncle Dewey was cackling so hard he would occasionally stomp the floor. When I came out, everyone tried to restrain himself but couldn't, and the laughter started again. I shouted, "What on earth's so funny?" Uncle Dewey finally got control, wiped the tears from his eyes, and said, "Hoyt and I saw you running through those briars and bushes like a jackrabbit and slapping at those bees. It scared us at first, 'cause we saw you'd been stung, but when you reached the field and were still running we figured you were OK. What a sight that was!" Then everybody started snickering again. I was not embarrassed. Actually I was pleased to be the center of attention.

All of us had been so engrossed in our jabbering about our honey harvest that we hardly noticed that the sun had slipped out of sight behind the trees, leaving us in the dark. Brother sniffed the night air and questioned, "What's that smell?"

"We all smell it, son. It's comin' from the kitchen, and it makes all of us hungry. I could eat a dead mule," declared Uncle Dewey.

Hoyt mumbled, "I think we can all agree with you on that."

Everybody got quiet, and with the silence on the porch I noticed that the bullfrogs down on the creek began to croak and the crickets' chirping grew louder. All of us were quiet, each thinking his own thoughts.

Aileen, Uncle Dewey's oldest daughter, finally came to the front door and announced, "If anybody's hungry, supper's ready." She didn't have to say that but one time. The famished menfolk (we children liked to think of ourselves as men) stumbled over one another, going through the dark living room on our way to the dining room.

The table was set for six people: Hoyt and Brother on one side, Dewey Lee and I on the other, Uncle Dewey at one end, and Aunt Lillian at the other. The girls—Aileen, Betty Lou, and Nancy—always had to wait for the second seating if there wasn't room at the table the first time around.

A red-and-white-checkered oilcloth was the tablecloth. The white tablecloth was used only on Sundays when the preacher was invited to dinner. An old, oil-wick kerosene lamp, the only source of light, decorated the center of the table. In the dim flickers of the lamp, we could see a bowl of rice, a plate of middling meat, a pan of hot biscuits, and a dishpan brimming full of honeycomb with about three inches of pure honey which had leaked from the comb to the bottom of the pan.

Our mouths watered as we anticipated that first bite, but we had to wait for Aunt Lillian's signal to begin. Finally it came. "Dewey, ask the blessing."

"Thank the Lord for supper. Amen," prayed Uncle Dewey fervently, and we all fell to passing the bounty and filling our plates.

I was just about to dip my biscuit in the golden, succulent fruit of our labors when Uncle Dewey cautioned, "Watch out for the dead bees!" I looked down in my plate and was shocked to see five or six little black bees decorating the honey in my plate. This was a seven-year-old's first encounter with wild honey. Aunt Lillian saw my surprise and told me, "Just rake the bees to the side of your plate."

"If you eat one, it won't hurt you. As a matter of fact, I heard bees may be good for you," Uncle Dewey added.

Aunt Lillian cut in. "Don't be telling him such nonsense."

"No, really, I heard eating bees may be good for you." Who knows? Uncle Dewey, ahead of his time, could have heard something about protein.

Anyway, along with the others, I raked the dead bees from the honey to the side of my plate and said, "Pass the biscuits."

We all ate with relish, and, when we had finally finished, we pushed back our chairs, sighing with contentment. It wasn't long before we again began congratulating ourselves on our superior honey harvest, and of course Uncle Dewey reiterated his tale of me running through the briars like a jackrabbit. Aunt Lillian interrupted him saying, "I heard you on the porch, teasing Tommy. Well, Dewey, I didn't hear you talking about *you* running through the briars. You must've done somethin' to tear your pants all to pieces. I'm glad you had on two pairs of pants. If you hadn't, you would've been nekkid. And, by the way, how did you get that briar scratch on the left side of your face? I really don't think you could've run like a jackrabbit, but you certainly must've walked mighty fast." I knew she was trying to take up for me, but it wasn't necessary. I was still enjoying the notoriety.

Everyone was quiet, waiting for Uncle Dewey's reaction. A minute passed as he studied the situation. But then Uncle Dewey burst out laughing, and everybody joined in.

Finally Hoyt said, "I certainly enjoyed the supper, the day, and everything. And I'd like to stay longer, but I need to go home." He left, and pretty soon we all piled on to beds if we could find an empty one or pallets spread on any available floor space. Soon we were sleeping soundly. I really don't believe I could do that now.

The day of the honey tree was history. And, sadly, the day of the wild honeybee in my area is history. There are no hollow limbs on stately oak trees, no homes for the bees where timber companies have clear cut, and two-story houses stand where honeybees used to buzz. In addition, diseases and insects have almost destroyed the wild honeybee and are now invading the hives of the domesticated bees. Beekeepers and scientists are working to find ways to save these busy creatures, which pollinate our food supply.

But there is one certainty. The memory of the day of the honey tree will live with me forever.

CHAPTER FIVE

Deans School

BEFORE I KNEW IT, the summer of 1934 had passed, and the month that all of us children hated was upon us. You guessed right, September. It was time for us to consent to being confined in what we called prison: the schoolhouse.

You will recall that I attended first grade in Nashville. Moving back to the home place entitled me to go to Deans School with my friends, an improvement, or so I thought. Daddy knew better. What a surprise was in store for me. My buddy, Allen Cooper, still lived on Evans Road, which was not far from my new home on the path. He, Dewey Lee, Brother, the whole gang, and I had played together, but this was the first time since I moved back home that I was to join them at school.

The First Day

ON THE FIRST DAY of school, I learned something about real country folks and their schooling. We arrived so early that first morning that the schoolhouse was still locked. There were several other children already there in the schoolyard. I had previously been told that my second-grade teacher was Miss Deany Card, who I secretly hoped would be as nice as Mrs. White, my first-grade teacher.

Feeling a little tug on my overalls, I turned around to find little Creech Whitley. He eagerly looked up at me and said, "I'm goin' to school, too. I'll be in the first grade." Creech looked a little nervous. He lived around the V near my Aunt Nettie. The V, now named Rose Loop Road, formed a half-circle beginning and ending on Old Bailey Highway. I've always wondered why we didn't call it the U.

Creech wasn't a stranger, but because he was younger, he wasn't in my close circle of friends. This morning, he had a fresh haircut, one that our community called a bowl cut. A bowl was actually placed on your head, and your hair was trimmed around up to the edges of the bowl, leaving a mop of hair on top. This was the only cut large families could afford, but, being an only child, I got my haircuts from the Nashville barbers, Lonnie Brake or Chinaman Ferrell. I never knew Chinaman's real name. Having a neat haircut was a priority with my daddy. Even after I was a grown man, he would offer me money if "you can't afford to get a haircut."

In spite of the hot September weather, Creech wore a ragged sweater with sleeves so long they flapped at the end of his fingers. His overalls were ragged; the knees and the seat of his pants had holes dotted here and there. Not that we were without patches, but little Creech looked like a rag doll. Feeling a little sorry for him, I said, "Creech, who's your teacher?"

He quickly responded, "Miss Card."

Not wanting him to feel bad, I gently questioned, "Are you sure? I thought she was my teacher."

"Naw. She's mine," retorted Creech.

"OK," I answered, and I just left it there, understanding that Creech, being a first-grader, probably didn't know.

I went back to Allen and Dewey Lee, standing nearby. Allen asked, "Where've you been?"

"Over talking to the little Whitley boy, poor fellow. He doesn't even know who his first-grade teacher is. He thinks it's Miss Card."

"It is," said Allen.

"Is what?"

"Yes, Miss Card *is* his first-grade teacher," shouted Allen, no doubt thinking I was beginning to lose my hearing.

"Well, my friend, who is our second-grade teacher?" I angrily retorted.

"Why, Miss Card!"

I was dumbfounded. Was someone playing a trick on me? I turned to Joyce Ayers, who had just walked up and was, I knew, in the third grade. Laughing sarcastically, I asked, "Who's your teacher, Joyce? Miss Card?"

Without cracking a smile, she looked at me strangely and responded, "Yes."

Three shocks in a row. One teacher for grades one, two, and three. But, believe me, I had more shocks to come. Scratching my head, standing there in the schoolyard, I pondered the one-teacher, three-grade situation. How on earth is Miss Card going to handle teaching three grades at once? If she puts each grade in a room, will she run back and forth from room to room? When she leaves a room, who will keep us quiet?

Finally, the school door opened, and everybody trooped in. There was no bell at Deans School. Some students went in one room, and I followed Dewey Lee and Allen to the other room. I noticed that

Brother didn't go with us. He went in the first room; he was in the fourth grade.

As I walked in I noticed that little Creech and Joyce were already there. "Well," I said to myself, "we haven't been separated yet."

All of a sudden, everybody got quiet. I turned. There stood a young woman with jet black hair and brownish-green eyes. Her long, pale blue dress, which hung about six inches from the floor and clung delicately to her slender frame, made her look taller than she probably was. I thought she was the most beautiful woman I had ever seen.

I leaned over my desk as far as I could, trying to look around her to see if Miss Card was in sight. At that instance I heard Joyce Ayers, who was sitting in a front desk, softly say, "Good morning, Miss Card."

I was in a state of shock. *Well,* I thought, *she certainly doesn't look like Miz White.* Not to say that I didn't like Mrs. White—I loved her—she was the motherly type. I was soon to learn that Miss Card really wasn't the motherly type.

Allen, Dewey Lee, and a boy who lived around the V, Roger Cockrell, had been playing marbles outside. They were now in the back of the room arguing about who won which marble. They were yelling at each other and were so engrossed in their argument that they had not seen Miss Card enter the room. She walked to her desk and turned to the blackboard, then turned again to the classroom, pointing at us with a yardstick she had retrieved from the little chalk shelf that ran along the bottom of the blackboard. All this seemed to happen in slow motion. But not for long. Suddenly she raised the yardstick over her head and slammed its flat surface on the wooden desk. It sounded like a shotgun blast. The brown had faded from Miss Card's brownish-green eyes. Allen, Dewey Lee, and Roger scrambled for the nearest desks.

Miss Card walked around in front of her desk. Her icy green eyes pierced each of us in turn, and with a voice suddenly encased in steel she said, "There will be order in this classroom. There will be no scuffling, fights, or loud noise. You will, I say *will*, act like ladies and gentlemen. I do not intend to spend my time on disciplinary problems. Have I made myself clear? Are there any questions?" Needless to say, there were none.

I was numb with fear. I had never heard Mrs. White talk that way. A few minutes passed with complete silence in the classroom until Miss Card continued, "Now, students, I know that you think I'm a mean person, but I'm not. I love children, and I enjoy teaching, but no teacher can teach anybody anything in a rowdy schoolroom, particularly when you have to teach three grades at once in one room. You deserve better, and I hope that the Nash County Board of Education will someday realize it."

Good Lord, teaching the first, second, and third grades in one room. How can she do it? I thought. Then I began to understand that it was a necessity for a teacher to maintain discipline in a classroom. I was no longer afraid of her. I fell in love with her all over again. Throughout my whole school life, I never forgot this lesson. I guess this was one of the reasons I never gave any of my teachers any trouble. Of course the fact that my mother told my teacher, "If you have to whip him just let me know and I'll whip him again when he gets home" might have had something to do with my good behavior. As a matter of fact I admired all my teachers—some more than others, of course. But not everyone agreed with me about Miss Card, declaring that she was just too bossy.

"All right," Miss Card began, "I want to welcome all of you back to school, and a special welcome to you first-graders. How does it feel to be grown up and be in school just like other children?" I could visualize the little ones sticking their chests out with pride. She continued, "And I would like to introduce Tommy Cooper, who last year completed the first grade in Nashville Elementary School. We welcome you, Tommy. Please stand up."

I was shocked again. I stood up so quickly that I hit my pencil against my desk, causing it to sprint across the floor. Thanks to Miss Card's great discipline, nobody giggled.

With all the ups and downs, new people, new school, excitement, shocks, and new teacher, my emotions were in turmoil. After being introduced, I sat down at my desk and began to feel a little better, but disaster waited. I had a pressing need to go to the bathroom. I wriggled around, trying to alleviate the uncomfortable urge, but to no avail. I prayed that someone in the classroom would raise his hand and ask to be excused, but no one did.

Finally my bladder conquered my embarrassment. I slowly raised my hand. Miss Card looked at me questioningly, "Yes?"

I blurted out, "May I go to the bathroom?"

Miss Card, recognizing my unease, smiled and gently said what I had prayed for her to say, "Yes, you may."

I meekly arose from my desk and quickly went out of the room and into the hall. *Where's the bathroom*? More specifically, *Where's the boys' bathroom?* I asked myself. I looked up and down the short hall. There were five doors: the first led to my room; the next door, I knew, led to the fourth-, fifth-, and sixth-grade room; the third door led to the outside; the fourth and fifth doors were close together near the outside door. *Hooray! One for girls and one for boys,* I rejoiced. By this time a real emergency existed. I rushed toward the doors. Which one was the boys' bathroom? There were no signs over either door. In a frenzy, I grabbed the doorknob to the door on the right and jerked it open. Did my eyes deceive me? There in front of me were mops, brooms, stacked boxes. A storage closet! Leaving this door slammed against the wall, I rushed to door number five and, panic filling my heart, again grabbed the doorknob and jerked the door open. No! Mops, brooms, stacked boxes. Another storage closet! By this time, horror invaded my body. I simply had to go to the bathroom. I stifled a sob. *You stupid idiot*, I said to myself. *Go outside!*

As I turned to run, the fourth-fifth-sixth-grade room door opened, and out walked a fifth-grade student whose name I later learned was Bruce Tyson. He looked at me with a startled stare and asked, "What on earth's the matter with you?"

"The bathroom, the bathroom. I gotta go real bad," I sobbed.

"Well, what in the world are you doing in here in the hall? Hurry and come with me," replied Bruce.

He took me by the hand and ran so fast that I was like a sheet hanging in the wind. We, or should I say he, ran back behind the school house along a narrow path that led through a few pine trees to a small, wooden, rectangular structure situated over a hole in the ground. The boys' bathroom! I flung open the door; I believe I actually flew inside.

Words cannot describe my relief. I clasped both hands together, placed them under my chin, tilted my head back, and uttered, "Thank you, Lord, thank you. And this time I really, really mean it."

Bruce, almost out of breath, observed, "You *must* be the new boy. Welcome to Deans School."

"Thank you. Thank you. Thank you. You're my friend forever. I'll never ask you for anything, and if I can ever help you, I will. But, Bruce, there's one more thing. Will you promise me you'll never tell anyone about this?"

Bruce smiled and said, "I promise."

I later heard that Bruce, when asked "Have you met Tommy?" replied, "Yes, when I met him he asked me to race him to the bathroom and, you know, the little scutter won!" He had altered the story just enough to keep his promise.

Many years later, I heard that Bruce had graduated from the University of Virginia, majoring in pharmacy, and that he had a good job working for a drugstore in Richmond. Every time I think of him, I think of our race to the bathroom and his promise not to tell. The rest of the day passed without incident, and I settled in to the routine of my new school.

Extracurricular

AFTER MY BATHROOM learning experience, I became more confident and comfortable at my new school, but there were still some things that I had to get used to.

There were no basketball hoops or basketballs, no slides, swings, or other exercise equipment. The baseball field was a small, broom straw field. We never played baseball, but we did play a game called Straight Cat. To play this game we were supposed to have a baseball, but we didn't have one; instead we used a ball made by winding tobacco twine into a round soft ball. Tobacco twine was the string we used to tie tobacco leaves to the sticks that were hung in the tobacco barn to cure. To make the ball a little harder we wrapped tape around it—if, of course, we could find any tape.

The players of the game consisted of the pitcher, the catcher, the batter, and as many fielders as came to play. There were only two bases: the pitcher's mound and home plate where the catcher was located.

If the pitcher struck the batter out or threw him out before he ran to the pitcher's mound and back to home plate, then the batter was out. In that case the batter became the pitcher, and the pitcher took the batter's place. If the batter hit the ball to a fielder, who caught the ball or threw the ball to the catcher before the hitter could run to the pitcher's mound and back to home plate, the batter was out; and the batter took the fielder's place so that the fielder could become the next batter. Whenever the batter hit the ball and was able to run to the pitcher's mound and back to home plate without being thrown out, the batter got to hit again, for as long as he could continue to be successful. I can't remember anybody keeping score. It was enough to be able to continue batting.

Straight Cat was played mostly by fifth- and sixth-graders, but anybody could play, and I did. I never saw a girl playing Straight Cat. Their games were hide-and-seek, hopscotch, jump rope, and jackrocks.

We boys didn't stick to Straight Cat. We played marbles, Stick Frog, and sometimes we even joined the girls for a round of hide-and-seek.

Stick Frog, a game played with pocketknives, was one of my favorites. When I was young, every boy I knew had at least one pocketknife, which was a small knife with blades that folded into the handle. I had three or four, thanks to Santa Claus, who always had an unlimited supply in his sleigh at Christmas. Although kids sometimes fought on the school ground, I never heard of anyone getting cut or even using a knife in a fight. And there was no school rule against carrying a pocketknife!

The object of Stick Frog was to get your knife to stick in the ground a certain number of times using various, increasingly difficult methods. A failure at any point disqualified the player. The last man standing was, of course, the winner. First, the player stood up, took the blade between the forefinger and the thumb, and flipped it to the ground three times, making it stick each time. Those who survived the first round went on to round two. Next, the player held the knife by the blade point, just under the nose with the head tilted forward. After nodding the head up and down several times, the player flipped the knife, sticking the point in the ground. This feat, once again, had to be accomplished three times. Next the successful player formed a hole by holding the forefinger and thumb together and then dropped the knife through the hole three times.

If the knife stuck each time, the player could then move to another, more difficult position called jumping the fence. He placed one hand vertically on the ground like a small fence, placed the handle in his other hand and tried to flip the knife over the fence. Anyone who could stick the knife three times in this position deserved to be the winner. As to the name of this game, I have no idea how the frog got in Stick Frog.

I know that many of my readers remember how to play these games, but my grandchildren probably never heard of them. Since my Deans School experiences took place in the 1934 Depression year, we had to figure out ways to amuse ourselves that didn't cost much.

One day at lunchtime recess, Allen, Roger, and I strolled over to where Dewey Lee, Brother, and James Rackley were crouched on the ground in a circle, about to start a game of marbles. Dewey Lee shouted out, "Y'all come on over. We're about to start the game." They had already drawn a circle in the dirt.

James said, "Hey, since we have six players, let's just put two marbles each in the ring. That'll make twelve marbles in all. Come on, you guys, ante up. Let's go."

Roger complained, "You and Dewey Lee are the best marble shooters in this school."

Allen piped up, "Well, come on, what the heck? It'll be just two marbles you can lose."

Allen and I dropped in two marbles. Roger fumbled in his

pockets and finally dropped his two marbles in. Dewey Lee marked a straight line in the dirt and then took nine steps and marked another line. All of us knew that we would toe the first line and toss our marbles as close as we could to the other line. The marble closest to the line would get the first shot and so on down the line. If there was a tie, of course they would toss again to break the tie. The order of the shots thus determined, the game began. Dewey Lee, of course, earned the first shot.

Roger yelled, "See, what'd I tell ya! You can't even beat him tossin' closest to the line!"

Dewey Lee looked up and with a deep sigh retorted, "It was just luck."

"Naw, it won't. Go ahead and shoot," Roger answered back.

We all got down on our knees around the ring. Dewey Lee had his big marble, called the log cart, ready for the first shot, laying his right hand on the ground and smoothly and expertly closing his hand over the log cart so that it could roll between his thumb and index finger. Tension built. All eyes were fixed on Dewey Lee's hand when the big glass sphere exploded into the group of marbles we had placed in the ring. One of them rolled quickly out of the ring, while the log cart stuck right in place as Dewey Lee had intended. When that happened, the shooter got another go and could continue until his log cart, too, rolled out of the ring. Dewey Lee won three marbles before any of the rest of us could have a chance to shoot.

After a lot of shooting and yelling, the game ended. Dewey Lee had eight of the twelve marbles. Poor Roger lost both his marbles, and so did I. Roger was right after all.

We played for keeps. The marbles you won were yours. My mother never knew this. To her that would have been gambling and, therefore, a sin. Needless to say, I did not enlighten her.

Before we knew it, the warmth of sunny fall days had evaporated into the chill of Old Man Winter. Our outside games were greatly diminished, and, of course, we had no indoor gyms.

I remember the cold mornings, the ground frozen hard, frost sprinkled on the dead grass, and ice in the schoolyard mud holes. We stood around, blowing our hot breath into our hands to keep them warm, turning up our coat collars and snapping the earflaps of our Lindbergh caps to keep out the frigid air, waiting for the school door to open. When it did, we rushed in to stand around the old coal-burning stoves, pushing slyly for our spot in the welcome warmth. There were no radiators that were placed around the room to spread the heat like we had back at Nashville School.

The best I can remember, there were two stoves at Deans: one in the first-, second-, and third-grade room, and one in the fourth-, fifth-, and sixth-grade room. Each stove was placed on a thick layer of dirt, which was enclosed in a square made of boards about eight inches high. If a hot coal fell out of the stove, it would fall harmlessly into the dirt. These stoves, fed by coal, would get red hot. Our teachers were always admonishing us not to get too close or our clothes might catch on fire.

I do not remember ever seeing a janitor at the school. I do remember that the boys in the fourth-, fifth-, and sixth-grade room were assigned the task of bringing in the coal from the coal pile outside. On occasion these boys actually started the fire in the stove, but most of the time it was the job of the teachers. Sometimes our overburdened teachers had this task done for them by Mr. John Deans, who lived about one hundred yards across the road from the school. He would have made a fine PTA president had there been such a thing then.

As a matter of fact, the following summer, Mr. Deans, my daddy, and some other community members petitioned the Nash County

Board of Education to consolidate Deans School with Nashville Elementary School. After hearing an effective litany of three grades in one room with one teacher, no equipment, coal-burning stoves, and so on, the board agreed. I'll never forget John Deans standing at the well with Daddy and me drawing water. He had a grin on his face. "Roy," he said, "we did it. The board accepted our petition. The kids are going to Nashville School next year." Perhaps that was one of the sparks for my interest in politics! By working together and convincing government leaders, you can make a difference in people's lives. This is just as true today as it was then.

Although all of us were excited about attending Nashville School, none of us ever forgot the friendships we formed at Deans School. J. H. Deans, one of John Deans's children, became a hospital administrator in Winston-Salem. Whenever he visited Nashville, he would stop by my office, and we would always end up talking about old times and our life at Deans School. Roger Cockrell, Allen Cooper, and I became known as the three musketeers. We were always together throughout school, graduated from high school together, and went to Oak Ridge Military Academy together. Roger then split and went to Chapel Hill, but Allen and I spent our college life at Wake Forest. Miss Card would have been proud.

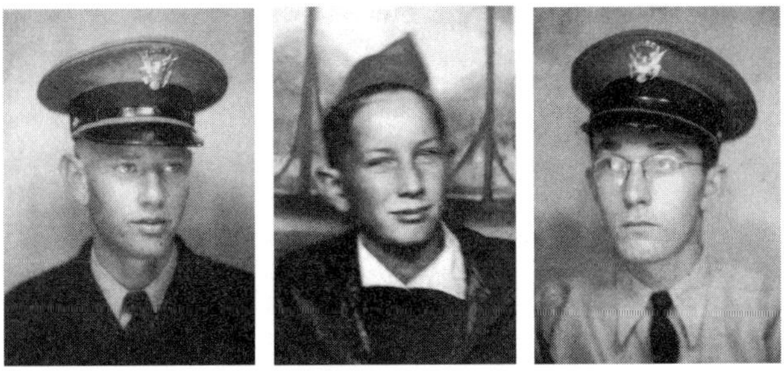

Allen, Roger, and Tommy
The three musketeers at Oak Ridge Military Academy

CHAPTER SIX

Neighborhood Parties

GROWING UP in the 1920s and 1930s, the Depression years, was a difficult time for the entire country, but it was particularly hard for country folks. There were big families, much work to be done, and little money to buy food or clothes or to hire anyone to help with the farming chores. Of course welfare was available, but in my neck of the woods farm families were a proud people, too proud to accept help from the government. In fact, people thought that the worst insult one child could fling at another was "Your mama's on welfare!"

Our neighborhoods were innovative. If the task was too difficult for one family to tackle alone, they simply invited the whole neighborhood over for a party, and everyone, even the children, pitched in. The work got done, and, as they say, a good time was had by all. We had hog killings, sawings, and corn shuckings, to name a few. As I look back over my childhood memories, I realize what an exciting part of my life these gatherings were.

CHAPTER SEVEN

Cracklins and Sweet Potatoes

I PEEPED OUT the back door. The night was pitch black. The stars were so bright you could see them twinkle. The ground was frozen solid. I was excited, maybe more excited than I was at Christmas a month before. In my bare feet and long underwear, I skipped through the kitchen on the cold linoleum to the warm sitting room where the little tin heater was red hot, puffing like a train. Daddy and Mother were sitting in their rocking chairs by the heater. I could hardly contain my enthusiasm. "It's fair and cold," I nearly shouted, knowing that's the kind of weather we needed.

Daddy looked up from reading the *Progressive Farmer* and said with a half-smile, "I reckon the hog killing's on."

"Time to go to bed," Mother added. "It's past eight o'clock."

I jumped up to open the door to the freezing bedroom and skipped back across the linoleum floor, dived into the bottomless feather bed, and sank so deeply that only my nose stuck out. Tomorrow was hog killing day. It was Saturday and no school. My parents would never let me miss a day of school. All the neighbors would come. I could hardly wait for morning.

It seemed the minute I closed my eyes our old Rhode Island red rooster sounded his regular morning alarm with a screeching *erc, erc, erch*. I looked over at Mother and Daddy's bed. We were back to one bedroom at the home place. Of course, they were already up. I bounded out of bed and ran into the dining-sitting room to find the old heater red hot and the wonderful smell of country ham permeating the house.

I pulled on a wool shirt and, of course, long underwear and soft, thick socks. Next I stepped into my "overhalls." We had never heard the words "dungarees" or "jeans." It took just a minute to tie the laces to my worn, but comfortable brogans, and I was ready for the hog killing. In the kitchen I found the dipper in the old wooden water bucket, frozen tight in the ice, another sign that it really was hog killing time.

After a hearty breakfast of country ham, hot biscuits, redeye gravy, and molasses, Daddy and I were off to make sure the hogs were in their fattening pen, where limited space and heavy feeding made the meat tender and the extra fat made more lard for cooking.

Next we made sure the water was in the vat, a rectangular wooden box lined with tin. After filling the vat with water, we started a fire in a hole under the vat. The water had to be very hot to facilitate the de-hairing of the dead hog. Not a pretty picture, but necessary for clean hog meat. The wash pot was next, and by the time we had filled the pot with water and built a fire around it, Uncle Brad, Uncle Bob, Uncle Jode, a man we called Uncle Captain, and the rest of the neighbors began to arrive. Most of the men in the community were called "uncle," as you notice. The women were called "aunt." Why some men rated "mister" I have no idea.

The women headed for the kitchen, and the men gathered around the fires at the wash pot and vat, trading jokes and warming their icy hands. Uncle Brad, of course, was purposefully sharpening his favorite butcher knife, holding it with his right hand and with his left sweeping it back and forth on the whet rock, which was a small slate rock used for sharpening. He was the one who gutted the hogs.

"Well," said Daddy, "let's get to it." Off we went to the hog pen. I ran on ahead to get Old Mary, our mule. I had already harnessed her to the slide truck, which would be used to transport the dead hog, the first of three. But I ran on ahead so that I could get to the pen before the kill in spite of instructions to arrive with Mary *after* the kill.

Uncle Jode was already aiming his .22 rifle, and Mr. Van (one of the few men in the community I called "mister"; I don't know why) was holding a sharp knife, standing in the pen waiting for the kill. A shot rang out, and the hog fell to its knees. Mr. Van ran, pushed the hog over, and with his right hand plunged the knife in the hog's throat, pulling the knife until there was a long slit. The blood flew. Old Mary, startled by the shot, jerked the rope out of my hand and ran off, slide truck and all, down in the pasture with me in pursuit. In a matter of minutes I caught her and returned her to her place beside the pen so that the men could load the hog on the slide truck, which would transport the dead animal to the vat. Unfortunately I was not quick enough. Daddy yelled at me, "I told you to keep that mule and yourself away from the pen. You know better!" Daddy never did like for me to be at the pen to see the shooting and gruesome throat cutting, but somehow I always managed to be there.

Old Mary leaned into the harness, and we were on our way to the vat, all the men at the pen following behind us. We needed at least four men to unload the hog, which weighed close to 250 pounds.

Uncle Brad and Daddy put a chain under the hog's shoulders, and Uncle Captain and Uncle Jode placed a chain just above the back legs of the hog. They then lowered the carcass into the scalding water and rolled it back and forth until Uncle Brad called out, "Over here, men. Need some help. It's ready!" About that time, to everyone's surprise, Sam Cooper, a big man about six feet tall and too fat for his apron overalls, pulled his brown, turned-up felt hat down over his eyes, walked up, and without a word came over quickly and helped pull the hog out of the vat and onto a large bench. Everyone in the neighborhood called him Bear Sam because he would go into the woods and disappear for months at the time. His reappearance was always sudden and unexpected. Speculation as to his activities in the woods was rampant. Some thought he made whiskey, an unfounded charge that was never proven to be true. Others figured he just wanted to get away from it all, like a modern-day Daniel Boone.

All of the men crowded around and began scraping the hair off the hog. Each man had brought his own scraper (a little tin blade with a wooden handle). While they worked, the men laughed, told jokes, talked, usually all at once. The camaraderie was evident. Of course Bear Sam didn't have a scraper and was standing back a little from the group, shifting on one foot and then the other, watching the men work, his hands thrust deep into his pockets. He seldom joined in casual conversation, but today he seemed to want to be a part of the group. His quiet voice got everyone's attention. "I knowed a man who owned a mule that wouldn't eat hay, corn, or grass."

"Well," Uncle Brad responded, "What *did* he eat?"

Nodding his head gravely, Bear Sam answered, "The same thing you eat."

Everybody started chuckling, "Naw! Come on!"

"I swear to God the man said the way it started was he was feeding the hogs one day, and the mule came up and started nibbling the biscuits in the slop bucket and from then on the mule wouldn't eat nothing that mules usually eat. The man said he decided to let the mule try the biscuits, and the mule loved 'em. Next the old animal started eatin' cooked vegetables, and finally ham and fatback. I swear I heard that," Bear Sam declared.

"Sam, who told you that?" asked Mr. Van skeptically.

Bear Sam retorted, "I swear I heard that, and it was told to me as the truth. I just don't remember who it was that told me." Everyone was quiet for a few minutes and then burst out laughing. I saw Bear Sam smile, and I thought that for the first time he felt a part of the crowd. I started thinking about what he said.

After about thirty minutes, Daddy said, "You ready, Brad?"

"Yeah, let 'er swing," Uncle Brad responded.

Every man present, including me (I was probably in the way, but no one said so), lifted the hog up on the gallows with the hog's head hanging down. Its back legs were hanging by the heel tendons, which had been cut so that a hickory stick could be stuck through each back leg, thus making the hog hang upside down. Uncle Brad called for a washtub. While he was gutting the hog and I was holding the tub to catch the entrails, I said, "Uncle Brad, do you believe that mule ate the same food that you and I eat?" He stopped, looked at me, and said, "Sometimes it's hard to tell when someone's tellin' the truth or just tellin' a good story. Sometimes you just can't tell. But what I do when I'm trying to decide, I first ask myself, number one, who's doin' the talkin', and number two, does it sound reasonable?"

I asked, "Well, what'd you think about the mule eatin' what you and I eat?"

He smiled and replied, "You figure it out."

I thought about that mule story a long time. I had never heard of a mule eating human food. It didn't sound reasonable. I decided that it was just a tale or maybe just a real good joke. The Uncle Brad test worked.

After all the hogs had been gutted, it was time for the men to cut up the carcasses into hams, shoulders, spare ribs, and other body parts.

As soon as that job was complete, Daddy turned to me and said, "Go to the house and tell Lois to get the ladies out here. It's time for them to get to work on the chitlins." "Chitlins" is the country word for hog intestines, which are used to make that delicious country link sausage you had for breakfast. Cleaning the chitlins was a dirty job reserved for the women and children.

At about this same time, my friends and cousins started to arrive. Dewey Lee and Brother arrived first and cried out simultaneously, "Oh, no, not again. Every time we get here too soon. It's gut rinsin' time!" And it was.

The women all dipped hot water out of the wash pot into smaller pots. Mother and Aunt Ethel went over to the vat and started dragging Uncle Brad's "gut tub," which was so full of chitlins that they couldn't pick it up. Dewey Lee, Brother, and I rushed over to help them, and we struggled over to the field where Aunt Lillian, Aunt Addie, and Miss Rada were waiting with the hot water beside the holes that had been dug in the field. After dropping our load, Dewey Lee, Brother, and I started drifting toward the stables, but sharp-eyed Aunt Ethel brought us to a halt with "Come back here. You know what your job is!" And a dirty job it was.

Miss Rada grabbed an intestine, cut open one end, and dumped the excrement out into one of the holes. Oh, did it stink! She then held the gut open while Brother and I grabbed a pot of boiling water and poured it in the open end. Miss Rada clamped that end shut and then began the rinsing process . . . holding one end up and then down and up and down and then finally emptying the dirty water into the hole. This process was repeated by groups of women and children until all the chitlins were clean and frying-pan ready.

In the midst of this process, Allen, Thurston, Benjamin, and James came up the path together, but when they realized that their arrival was untimely, for them anyway, they turned and started to sneak away. Aunt Ethel's strident command stopped them. "You leave now and you get no cracklins!" That threat was too much for the boys, and they reluctantly joined us in the field to finish the "dirty work."

As soon as all the chitlins were cleaned, the women immediately began trimming the fat off the hog sections just cut up by the men while Mother went into the house to fetch a dishpan filled with freshly baked sweet potatoes. Each slab of fat was thrown into the wash pot to boil, where it dissolved into lard. The skin off the fat, bubbling toasty brown and crisp, rose to the surface of the lard to make cracklins. Aunt Ethel ladled the skins and placed them on a covered table, surrounded by children waiting expectantly, sweet potato in hand. "These cracklins are hot!" Aunt Addie yelled. "You young'uns are gonna get burned. Those skins just came out of that boiling grease!" As a matter of fact, some of us did get burned, but that was some good eating. I bit a soft juicy sweet potato and then crammed cracklins in my mouth until the grease ran out of the corners and down my chin. The "dirty job" was worth it.

With all the children's bellies full and all the meat salted down, it was time for the family friends to take some portion of the freshly killed hog meat and head for home. Tradition was that all the helpers got fresh hog meat for supper.

Before everybody said good-bye, Uncle Brad called out, "Well, folks, next Thursday, if nobody else is having one, I'll be doin' my hog killing, and y'all are all invited."

Not me, I thought. *Thursday's a doggone school day. But we get out at 3:30, and Uncle Brad's house is only a few yards down the path from the bus stop. Heck, I can make it there in time for cracklins!*

CHAPTER EIGHT

Sawings

SATURDAYS IN the wintertime! These were days for living! No school, no working in the fields, just fun: getting together with my playmates, playing cowboys and Indians, squirrel hunting, and tracking rabbits if it snowed. In addition to these pleasures, neighborhood parties were usually held on Saturday nights, and these parties weren't about watching a ballgame on TV with friends, cocktail parties, or bowling. You remember, neighborhood parties were held for the express purpose of getting a tough job done for one of the neighbors. But strangely enough, even though everyone worked hard, these get-togethers were always fun for all.

This particular Saturday, the "sawing" was to be held at the home of my granddaddy, Pa Fed. I jumped out of bed and ran from my cold bedroom to the dining/sitting room to find the little heater draft wide open, causing it to have a puffing sound. You could tell it was beginning to emit some pretty hot air when my dog Vanilla got up, stretched, and walked back to the old dining room table across the room to escape the heat and finish her nap. I dressed with unusual speed, grabbed a bite to eat, and headed out to Uncle Dewey's to spend the day in wide-open play, interrupted only by the occasional happy thought: *tonight's the sawing at Pa Fed's.*

When you're having fun, time flies, and it wasn't long before I was coming up the path, returning home to get ready for the big evening. The old oak trees in the yard were casting long shadows by the time I got back from Uncle Dewey's. I was tired, but when I saw Daddy on the front porch, filing his crosscut saw, fatigue was immediately flushed from my body. I was ready to go to the sawing.

We had an early supper. Mother had cooked Daddy's favorite food, which was fried ham, redeye gravy, grits, and my favorite, potato biscuits. Even though I liked everything on the table, I attacked the potato biscuits dripping with fresh churned butter as if I had not eaten all day long, and I hadn't. We had played so hard that I had completely forgotten to eat! Daddy finally said, "You keep that up and you won't eat a thing tonight. You know your grandmamma Lucy'll have pull candy, sea foam candy, peanut brittle, and chocolate fudge."

I looked up, my stuffed jaws poked out like a squirrel stuffing in hickory nuts for the winter, and replied, "Well, you know she never lets us eat anything until after the sawing. By then I'll have worked off every one of these biscuits and be ready to start on the candy."

Daddy and I finished eating, quickly pushed back our chairs from the table, and walked out on the front porch. Daddy picked up the crosscut saw he'd been sharpening, and I found the old kerosene lantern that would help light our way in the woods. After we had packed everything in the body of our old pickup truck, Daddy put his hands on his hips and called out to Mother, "We're ready!" Mother, hurrying to get the dishes off the table and into the dishpan, yelled back, "Be right there."

Soon Mother bustled out of the kitchen, and the three of us crawled into the truck. We were on our way to Pa Fed's.

All the men were on the porch or standing around under the giant oak trees in the yard when we drove up. "Hey, glad you made it," someone greeted us. Mother quickly joined the women who had already begun pulling sweet slabs of taffy, stirring pans of soft chocolate fudge, dropping spoons of airy sea foam on giant platters, and filling the night air with smells so delicious I immediately forgot all about those potato biscuits. I knew, though, that those pleasures were reserved for after the sawing and tried not to think about it.

My buddies were there, of course: Dewey Lee, Brother, Thurston, and Benjamin, to name a few. Like me, they were ready to go to the woods. They were jumping up, bumping into each other, when one of the men yelled, "OK, let's go! Let's get all the axes, saws, and lanterns together. If some of you have too much to carry, let's divide the things up so it won't be a burden on anybody. Hey! I almost forgot the files. Last time we had a sawing, nobody, I mean nobody, brought a file, and y'all remember how long it took us to finish with them dull saws!"

"Don't worry 'bout it. I brought two of 'em. I made shore that wouldn't happen again," Uncle Dewey assured him.

Wood was an absolute necessity in my early boyhood days. There was no electricity or gas to heat our homes, cook our food, wash our clothes, or cure our tobacco crops. And wood for each of these purposes had to be cut differently. Stove wood used to cook our food and heat our water, for example, had to be cut at shorter lengths than any other wood and split into narrow strips so that it would fit the cookstove. Of course this process required intensive labor and time and was actually the main reason sawings were necessary. Nobody had enough time to saw and split enough stove wood for the year. It took the whole neighborhood! Fortunately heater wood, fireplace wood, and barn wood were sawed in longer pieces and from smaller trees, requiring far less energy and saving the big pines for stove wood. Of course my daddy never in his life cut down a small pine tree unless it was crooked or diseased in some way. He knew the value of the big tall pines, although he never sold a tree!

We all shouldered our equipment and trudged through the field in front of Pa Fed's house to the woods where trees were lying in every direction where they had fallen. The trees to be sawed were usually cut down by the owner before the sawing, but Pa Fed at eighty was just too old. "Well, I don't know who cut down these trees, but whoever did this job knew what they were doing," Uncle Brad said after carefully looking over the fallen trees.

When the rest of us reached the site, we saw that most of these felled trees were laying one on top of the other, the bottom tree supporting the top one. This was done to keep the crosscut saw from jamming as it would when a log lying flat on the ground was cut to a certain depth and one or both ends of the log would rise up, the middle bending inward, closing the cutting area, and grabbing or, as we called it, biting the saw. The way these trees had been felled helped prevent that problem. The support of the bottom log held the top log open so that it wouldn't bite. As long as we could keep that top log supported, the crosscut saw would move smoothly through even the thickest tree trunk.

A crosscut saw was a sharptoothed blade about six feet long with handles on each end. To saw the wood, one man grasped the handle on one end of the saw, and another worker would grasp the other handle. Together they would pull the saw back and forth, back and forth until the blade had cut through the log. Was this a grueling, backbreaking job? You bet. It exercised every muscle in your body. We had never heard of a chainsaw. But, heck, if the chainsaw had made its appearance in my early boyhood days, there would not have been any neighborhood sawings, and I would have sorely missed those adventures. I am sure that the menfolk would probably disagree with the sawing part, but they would undoubtedly have missed the neighborhood party part.

We kids were the backup at these gatherings. Whenever sweating workers would get in trouble, they would yell for help. "Hey, you young'uns, come over here! Me and Clatie can't move this saw. It's stuck and we ain't even sawed through half the log. We need for y'all to bring that pole over yonder and use one of these blocks we've already sawed off."

Thurston, Benjamin, and I grabbed a pole and ran over to where Clatie and Roney were waiting, holding a crosscut saw hopelessly stuck halfway through a huge pine log, biting at its worst. Thurston and Benjamin jabbed the pole back and forth in the dirt until it was completely under the log where the saw had jammed. I rolled one of the blocks firmly under the pole near the tree trunk. The three of us grabbed the pole, lifted our bodies off the ground and hung over the pole, which pressed hard against the block, lifting the tree to a point where the saw tract gradually opened, freeing the saw so that Clatie and Roney could finish the job. If you don't think hanging in midair in the middle of the woods, bouncing up and down, and getting "Good job, boys!" for your efforts was great fun, you just don't understand!

Of course we didn't spend all our energy making life easier for the men. In fact, after we freed the saw, we decided we needed some playtime. I called all the boys together a few yards from where the men were hard at work, and in a half-whisper uttered, "Are y'all ready for racing some blocks down the hill?" Everybody agreed. The men were sawing tree trunks into round blocks of varying lengths depending on the use planned for the wood. Three feet long for stove wood, for example. They let the sawed wood lie where it fell, waiting for the owner to come in later and split it. These blocks were the racers in our dangerous, exciting game.

"We got to be mouse quiet this time," Allen warned us, "because the men found out all about them blocks being at the bottom of the hill when we had the last sawing at Uncle Dewey's. They said we better push them blocks back up or we would split them ourselves and haul 'em up the hill on a slide truck." Everybody nodded, agreeing to the chance we were taking. "I tell you what," Allen continued to whisper. "Let's just race four blocks down, two at a time, so we won't have to push so many back up the hill."

"Yeah," everybody agreed a bit too loudly.

"What are you young'uns up to?" Daddy asked suspiciously.

"Nothing!" Dewey Lee blurted out. "Just messing around."

That seemed to satisfy the grownups. We sneaked around the sawing area where the men had just finished and quickly rolled four round blocks some distance away to the top of the hill. For the first race, Allen and I got one block, and Thurston and Dewey Lee got a second block. On the count of three, we raced each other down the hill, each team rolling one block, ducking the trees, fallen tree limbs, briars, and other obstacles until we got to a predetermined finish line. Four more boys got two more blocks and raced the same course.

I can't remember who won, but I do remember that after the race we all sat on an old log to rest before trying to push those four blocks back up the hill. While we pondered the problem, the singsong of the saws and the chatter of the men floated down to us. Noise always travels farther and clearer in the woods, but after a few minutes the chatter seemed to be winning the voice race with the singsong of the saws. Sure enough, the saws fell silent. We could hear everybody talking at once.

Finally Uncle Brad shouted, "All right, let's take a fifteen-minute break."

"Where's the refreshment?" Roney demanded.

Benjamin whispered, "Can anybody guess what kind of refreshment Roney's talking about?'

"Oh yeah!" I snickered.

"Well, it sure ain't water." Allen started laughing, and the rest of us joined in. Dewey Lee laughed so hard, he almost fell off the end of the log.

"Wait, wait," Thurston broke in. "I betcha I know exactly what they're drinking. Y'all remember them barrels of cider we found under the barn shelter? We cut a hollow reed and stuck it in the hole in the barrel and sucked. You remember. Boy, won't it good! It made us a little dizzy, but it felt good."

"Not me! Tasted like vinegar with sugar in it." I grimaced a bit, remembering.

Thurston looked a little pensive. "Tommy, how come your daddy never joins in the liquor drinking?"

"I seen him when he was real drunk around Christmastime," Dewey Lee broke in.

"Well, is that the only time? Almost everybody drinks at Christmas," Thurston persisted, looking at me for an answer.

I pondered the question for a moment. "Well, you know, my daddy actually chooses the times when he wants to drink. Sometimes he does, and sometimes he doesn't. I guess he's just a strong-willed man."

The conversation drifted then to other topics, but I continued thinking about Daddy and the drinking question. I never thought of him as an alcoholic. Still don't, but every year at Christmas and sometimes when he had a good tobacco sale in the late fall he took a few weeks vacation, relaxing in the alcohol glow he denied himself on other occasions. You can imagine Mother's opposition to this practice even though it was, I do believe, his only vice. I always thought that only death would stop his yearly sprees. Well, death didn't stop it, but birth did. During Daddy's normal Christmas celebration, the December before the birth of his first grandson, he told my wife Beverly that he would never touch another drop. He didn't want anything to interfere with his time with "the boy." I laughed at his promise because I didn't think he'd stick to it. But he proved me wrong. As of June 13, 1957, the birth date of his first grandchild, until his death on October 13, 1970, he never touched another drop of alcoholic beverage.

Up on the hill the men grew louder, the longer the rest period lasted, until Uncle Brad hollered, "OK, OK, enough! Let's get back to work and finish sawing these trees." Everybody followed orders, and the singsong of the saws began again.

"Everybody's working hard. Maybe we should push these blocks back up the hill," Brother said. Racing down the hill with blocks almost as wide as the path had been dangerous but exciting. The return trip threatened to be backbreaking.

"How did we get these big blocks between those trees and around all those curves?" Thurston shook his head in amazement.

We began to struggle to the top. Ben was the oldest and boldest and the first to get hurt. About a third of the way up, his feet flew out from under him on the slick pine straw. Thankfully the injury was only skin-deep scrapes and bruises, if you didn't count the serious blow to his pride.

Getting those four blocks back up the hill was a long, slow process, but after about an hour we reached the top exhausted. It doesn't take young'uns long to bounce back, and we did just that when we saw that the men had finished sawing the last log and were collecting saws, axes, mauls, and other tools. They were getting ready to return to Pa Fed's where the women were waiting to serve their menfolk with parched peanuts, popcorn, and candies of all kinds. The women always added peanuts and popcorn because somehow they knew that not all of the men would want sweets after their clandestine "nips" in the woods.

It was nearly one o'clock in the morning when the party broke up, and Mother and Daddy got ready to leave. Daddy looked around for me but wasn't surprised when he opened the door of the old truck and found me stretched across the front seat, fast asleep.

As I now think back on those good old days, I wonder how many child labor laws were violated at these sawings: long hours into the night, dangerous conditions for underage workers, no pay. The time of fellowship and the satisfaction of a job well done made it worthwhile, though. Of course the love and that mouthwatering chocolate fudge are what I really remember!

CHAPTER NINE

My "Fodder" Adventure

OUR MAIN MONEY CROP was tobacco, followed by cotton. All other crops we planted were used primarily as feed for the farm animals and food for us, of course. A garden that had a few acres of sweet potatoes, Irish potatoes, and "roasting ear" corn provided prime ingredients for the tasty meals Mother prepared for us and for the farm workers.

Corn was by far the biggest crop used on the farm to feed the mules, cows, hogs, chickens, and, of course, us. Corn bread was a staple in those days. Although it didn't need as much labor as our money crops, corn required its share. We had to plant and chop until the corn was high and thick enough to defeat the ferocious weeds bent on gobbling up the fertilizer.

Fodder was a corn by-product that fed our mules. After the blades or leaves of the cornstalk were completely grown, we stripped them from the stalk, using one blade to tie the others into a bundle. We then hung each green bundle of blades on one of the ears of corn, where it would stay until it was completely dried by the sun into what we called fodder.

Tying fodder bundles was a skill I never developed. Every one I tied and hung unraveled, dropping its green blades to the ground. Needless to say, Daddy quickly decided to let me pull blades and hand them to someone better at that job. But depending on fodder to feed our mules was a risky business. If it rained before the bundles had completely dried and before we had hauled the fodder to the barn or stacked it in the field, it was ruined.

In fact, saving the fodder could be quite an adventure. I remember one night in particular even though I was only about eleven years old.

Daddy shifted in his rocking chair and folded the newspaper he had been reading. My dog, Vanilla, recognizing the signs, got up, yawned, and tiptoed across the linoleum floor to her favorite corner. "Time to go to bed. We got to get up early in the morning to get the fodder out of the field before it rains. We've had four good, hot days on it, and it's ready to get in," Daddy reminded us.

I ran and jumped into the bed. Mother and Daddy soon followed to the same room where we all slept, even though our house had four rooms. The almost unused living room, which Daddy had vainly suggested we convert to a bedroom, was always spotless, patiently awaiting the preacher's visit. Daddy always lost the argument when it came to household matters.

As soon as my head hit the pillow I was fast asleep. It seemed as though the very next moment Mother was shaking me. "Get up, Tommy, get up. Your Daddy and Sam have already gone down to the stables to catch the mules and hitch them to the wagon. It's lightning over toward Rada's, and we don't want the rain to ruin the fodder!" Mother was already mopping my forehead with a cold wash rag. Oh how I hated that cold rag in my face!

"But Mother, I just got in bed," I whined.

"No, son, it's one o'clock in the morning. You know Sam's the only one your daddy's got to help him. You've been sleeping since seven o'clock last night. Get up! I'm so sorry I have to get you up at this ungodly hour, but Daddy really needs you. Sam's the only one staying in the grading room this week. Thee won't get back until next week," Mother sadly reminded me. Sam Morgan and Thee were workers who regularly helped us on the farm.

I staggered out of bed, grabbed my overalls off the floor, and struggled to get one leg in. But the real trouble came when I lost my temper trying to get my other leg through the pants leg. I hopped across the floor on through the door and into the dining room, lost my balance, and hit the dining room table, knocking one of Mother's vases to the floor, smashing it into tiny pieces. Mother came running in from the kitchen.

"Oh my, are you hurt?" she asked, looking from me to the broken vase shards covering the floor.

I wasn't hurt, but seeing the look on her face changing from anxiety to anger, I pulled myself up and limped toward the kitchen.

"Did you know that Aunt Ola, who raised me from a tiny baby, gave me that vase?"

"Yes, Mother."

Mother finally regained her composure and asked if I could stand on my leg.

"Yes, Mother. I'm OK."

Well, I guess faking the hurt leg worked, I said to myself, as I quickly finished dressing. I knew Mother would value my welfare over an object, and because it was so early I didn't feel bad about it then. About that time I heard the unmistakable sound of the wagon coming from the mule stable up the path to our house on its way to the cornfield.

"Your daddy and Sam are almost in the yard. Here, take this ham and biscuit."

I rushed out and jumped on the wagon with Sam and Daddy. No one said anything except Sam, who said "Howdy" to Mother.

When we arrived at the field, Daddy began giving us instructions. "Tommy, you drive the mules and place the fodder bundles on the wagon and keep them packed down. We need to carry as big a load as we can each time. Sam and I'll throw the bundles on the wagon."

It was hard to see, and the lantern hanging on the wagon certainly was no match for the darkness. The night was unusually quiet. Evidently the frogs, crickets, night owls, and other normally noisy creatures of the night had stayed at home. They knew something we only suspected. A storm was coming. There was no moon, no stars, only darkness broken by staccato outbursts of light, like a faraway fireworks display.

Sam and Daddy stood up and looked toward the low-hanging clouds every few minutes. The flashes grew brighter, and the rumble of thunder began to break the silence of the early morning. Sam said, "Mr. Roy, I believe that cloud is comin' up."

"You may be right. Let's get the few bundles that are left on this row, and we'll head for the barn."

By the time the words got out of his mouth, a big, rolling boom like the voice of a cannon got our attention. The wind began to blow, bringing with it sheets of rain. Sam and Daddy jumped on the wagon with me and we huddled together, Daddy taking the reins. The mules, ears back and tails tucked between their legs, needed no driver. They turned and raced for the barn with bundles of fodder flying in every direction.

We sat under the barn shelter a long time before anybody spoke. Finally Daddy said with a sad smile, "You know, I think this is going to be my last year of trying to save fodder for the mules. Fodder rots if one drop of water falls on it, and a lot of people in the community have already stopped."

"Well, we've got enough oats planted this year to feed the mules, don't we?" I asked, hoping to give him some reassurance that everything would be all right.

"He sure is right, Mr. Roy. We got enough and then some." Sam was also trying to get Daddy in a better mood.

Smiling broadly, Daddy declared, "OK, at least we won't ever have to mess with fodder again." Now that was something to cheer about.

The rain soon stopped, and up walked Thee. Sam said, "Where you been? You sho knows when the work is over. I can tell you that."

"Mr. Roy knows that ain't so. I'm here most of the time when he needs me," Thee answered.

Sam said, "The only time you come around is when you need money."

Thee was only about five feet tall. He had broad shoulders and muscular arms, probably as a result of a lifetime of hard work. His skin was reddish brown, and he looked like he was smiling all the time because his thin lips were sort of stretched across his teeth. The faded blue jacket and overall pants that he always wore seemed to highlight his twinkling blue eyes. But his cap was the ugliest thing I ever saw, and he was never without it. It was very old with a narrow bill and a balloon-shaped head part that slipped over to one ear.

Sam and Thee unhooked the mules and turned them in the lot. Daddy and I trooped home in our wet clothes while Sam and Thee went to the grading room to get cleaned up.

As soon as I got on some dry clothes, I went to the grading room, as I often did, propped myself by the door, and began my usual interrogation. This time I picked on Thee. Some called him Thedo because his name, I guessed, was probably Theodore. Some folks called him Red. I figured that was because of his rust-colored skin. When I asked him about it, he smiled and said, "I sho ain't no Injun, and don't worry 'bout what my name is. When you call me to eat, you can call me anything." I never found out what his real name was or where he came from. I regret that I didn't pursue that conversation.

I learned a lesson from Daddy during this fodder episode, as I often learned from him. Work as hard as you can, but when adversity strikes, if there's nothing you can do about it, just smile and move on. That's certainly what he always did, and though I sometimes fail, I try to do the same.

CHAPTER TEN

Spirits in the Corn

CORN SHUCKINGS were not as common in our community as sawings, but they were almost as much fun.

One day just as the school bus rolled up to Aunt Pat's house at the end of the day, I jumped from my seat and started for the door before the bus stopped. The driver, Rachel Cooper, glared at me and demanded that I return to my seat until the bus came to a complete halt. Then she asked why I was in such a hurry. I told her that we were having a corn shucking. That, she smiled and explained, did not give me the right to jump off the school bus before it stopped, but she sure hoped I had fun. I apologized, bounded off the bus, and began to trot past Uncle Brad's, Uncle Bob's, up the hill ditches, and by Mr. Van's to my house.

As I came into the yard, I saw Uncle Dempsey, another one of our semi-regular workers who, along with Sam and Thee, "roomed" from time to time in the grading room. He had just returned after about a three-month absence. I ran over to meet him to tell him about the corn shucking, but he had already talked to Daddy. He had told Uncle Dempsey that the corn needed to be moved from the crib into the barnyard in three big piles arranged so that four shuckers would have room to work at each pile. My job was to spread the cotton sheets for the piles of corn.

When I went into the house to get my after-school snack, I saw that Mother had already started preparations for the corn shucking party planned for that night. The reddish-brown cookies were irresistible. My taste buds were working overtime as my hand involuntarily reached toward the dish of cookies, only to be stopped by a slap on the knuckles. "You may have a meat and biscuit, but cookies and candy are for tonight," she admonished me. Daddy smiled as he sat munching, you guessed it, one of those reddish-brown cookies. *Oh well*, I thought, *one of these days I'll be the man of the house.*

Daddy brushed the cookie crumbs off his shirt and gave me instructions to go down to the crib, spread cotton sheets, and help Uncle Dempsey get the corn out for the shuckers.

It didn't take me long to run down the path at the back of the house to the corncrib. I was already sitting in the crib door waiting when I heard the *clump, clamp* of Uncle Dempsey's hip boots as he ambled down the path. His mumbling was hard to decipher, but when he got nearer, I heard him say, "Rather have rats in the crib. Why don't he git some cats? Everybody *knows* they eat rats."

"What are you talking about, Uncle Dempsey?"

"Well," he muttered as he cautiously approached the crib door. He peeped inside, his eyes slowly roving over the corn and up toward the rafters at the top of the crib. His body reminded me of a coiled spring, ready to snap back at the slightest noise or movement. "I don't aim to get bit," he answered.

"I can't believe you're scared a rat will bite you."

"It ain't the rats that I'm scared of. It's them black snakes that Mr. Roy put in the crib!"

"Black snakes eat rats, they don't bite people! Have you ever heard of anyone being bitten by a black snake?" I retorted.

"Shore have. I heard of a man over at Sandy Cross that was bit by one, and it nearly killed him."

"Who told you that?"

"I don't know, but it was told for the truth."

"That's hard to believe, Uncle Dempsey. Black snakes are nonpoisonous, and I've never heard of anybody being bitten by a black snake."

Uncle Dempsey quickly shot back, "Well, I sho ain't never heard of anybody else catching black snakes and putting them in the corncrib. Have you?"

"I've heard of folks doing it to get rid of rats."

"Who?" Uncle Dempsey asked, glaring at me.

I wanted to answer, "I don't know, but it was told to me for the truth," but I didn't, deciding that a smart-aleck response wasn't appropriate. Instead, I said nothing. We both silently began to spread the cotton sheets as instructed and began emptying baskets of corn on the sheets, Uncle Dempsey ever alert for the friendly black snakes that lived in the crib.

Uncle Dempsey finally broke the silence. "Mr. Roy's a good man, and he's smart, got a good head on him. He's fair, expects us workers to work hard, but pays us good. The only thing is, I don't understand him putting all them black snakes in the crib. I tell you one thing, ain't nobody gonna steal no corn from this crib."

After about three hours and many trips to and from the sheets to the crib, Daddy walked up. "That's enough corn, boys. Good job.

Looks like it's gonna be a good night for the shucking. The weather's fair, and the moon will almost be bright enough for us to blow out the lanterns." He then told Uncle Dempsey to take the rest of the day off. "Go by the house," he instructed, "and tell Lois to put eight hours on the book for you. You've earned it."

Uncle Dempsey looked at me and nodded with a smile for he knew that Daddy had given him two hours as a bonus for this day's work. As he turned to go to the house, he stopped and said, "Mr. Roy, you is a fair man."

Daddy then looked at me. "You can go, too. I guess your bonus will be that cookie you didn't get this afternoon."

That night everyone had fun, the women all talking and laughing at once, and adding to Mother's array of cookies and candy; the men frantically shucking corn and searching for the bottle of spirits Daddy had hidden in one of the piles; the children at the stables arguing about who would be the sheriff or the outlaws; and everybody wanting to be the Lone Ranger. Another memorable neighborhood party!

CHAPTER ELEVEN

Ghost Light

It was the month of October. Halloween month. The nights were getting longer, giving the witches, goblins, and ghosts more time to creep around in the darkness. Even the grownups were beginning to tell stories of these creatures of the night, and this excitement occasioned a neighborhood party of a different kind.

On one such evening, a flock of us young'uns were—where else?—at Uncle Dewey's. The house was full. The grownups were back in the kitchen where the men were laughing and talking and drinking hard cider while the women were busily stirring steaming pots of pull candy.

With no electric lights, no TV, no radio, no stereo, and no movies, we children had to create our own amusement. We played spin the bottle, ring on a string, pick-up sticks, and other games you've probably never heard of.

In my day of growing up in the country, very few grownups had a formal education. I assume that was the reason most people were superstitious, a mind bent that provided fertile ground for the creation and telling of some mighty tall tales. When one of the adults began to tell a yarn, we children would give up the games we were playing and scuttle for the empty chairs, forming a ring around the storyteller. Those who failed to get a chair formed an inner circle sitting on the floor. These stories were usually told before a crackling fire in the big fireplace and the yellow flame of a little oil lamp on the mantle, barely eliminating the darkness and creating flickering shadows on the wall.

One of the best storytellers was Mr. Andrew Cockrell, and, on this particular October evening, when he strolled out of the kitchen and pulled a chair up to the fireplace, we children quickly dropped our pick-up sticks and scrambled excitedly to form a circle around him. We knew a good yarn was coming. He sat down saying, "Young'uns, you want to hear about Etta Mae and the ghost light?"

All of us children gave a resounding "*Yes!*"

Mr. Cockrell began.

"A long time ago there was a girl named Etta Mae. She was about twelve years old, had her hair cut short like a boy, seldom wore a dress. Most of the time she wore overalls and shirts, just like the boys. She could outrun, outfight the boys—in fact, do most anything the boys could do and do it better. And you know what? She was beautiful. And even though she put the boys to shame, all of them were secretly in love with her."

"I know a girl like that, 'cept she ain't pretty," Dewey Lee interrupted.

Two or three of the listeners shouted, "Shut up, Dewey Lee. Let Mr. Cockrell go on with the story."

Mr. Cockrell continued.

"Well, in the community where she lived there was an old graveyard in a field near the woods about one-half mile from where Etta Mae and her family lived. No one kept up the graveyard. Briars, honeysuckle vines, and scrub bushes almost covered the entire grave area, but some gravestones could be found in a mysterious circle where no vegetation grew. No one could understand why nothing would grow in this circle. Some said it was caused by the ghost light."

This time not only Dewey Lee, but almost everybody was raising or should I say waving hands and shouting, "What's a ghost light? What's a ghost light?"

"Young'uns, do you want me to finish the story or not?"

"Yes! Yes!" we all answered in unison.

"Well, nobody actually knows what a ghost light is, but the story goes this way. Once every Halloween night a strange light appeared between the hours of 10:30 p.m. and 11:00. No one could explain the light, and everyone was afraid to go out to the graveyard to see what it was. Finally one Halloween night a brave group of the neighbors got together and started out to the graveyard to try and find out the source of the light. They reached the edge of the cemetery and quietly waited. First 10 o'clock came, then 10:30. All of a sudden a yellowish, bright light slowly rose from the bare circle in the cemetery and drifted toward the open field, then across the field until it got to the woods. When it got to the woods it slowly rose up over the trees and floated out of sight. Someone in the crowd looked at his watch. It was exactly 11 o'clock."

"Is that all? What about Etta Mae?" the children wanted to know, all talking at once.

"My patience is growing thin. If I hear even a pin drop from any of you again, I ain't gonna finish the story." After that warning, if a pin had dropped, it would have made a loud thud. I believe that Mr. Cockrell was enjoying himself immensely. "Where was I?"

All the children yelled, "The light went over the woods!"

"OK," Mr. Cockrell smiled.

“The next year on Halloween night, the year after the neighbors had seen the light in the cemetery and after all of the children had listened wide-eyed to their story, the neighbors and all the children in the neighborhood got together just like us here tonight. Etta Mae was there. She was dressed, for a change, in a long white skirt and a red sweater. As usual she was beautiful. Everyone gazed at her, the boys, the longest.

“For some reason or other, the get-together didn’t go too well, and the children got bored. Suddenly, Etta Mae jumped up and hollered out, ‘I tell you what let’s do. Let’s all of us walk up to the cemetery. It’s almost ten-thirty, and it ain’t very long before we could see what that ghost light is all about.’

“Everybody stopped in their tracks; the silence was deafening. Believe it or not, a gust of wind rushed in, blowing out the oil lamp on the mantelpiece and blowing the fireplace ashes, causing the coals to turn red. The girls screamed. But everybody breathed a sigh of relief when the door shut and there stood one of the neighbors who was late for the get-together. He just smiled at the children and went on through to the kitchen.

“Etta Mae just ignored the newcomer and gave a highfalutin smile. She said, ‘Well, are y’all comin’ or not?’

“‘Ain’t nobody with good sense gonna go up to that graveyard on this night, and I’ll tell you Etta Mae ain’t either. She just wants everybody to *think* she’s so brave. There ain’t nobody here wants to go up to that cemetery, including her,’ said one of the big boys. His hands were on his hips, and his voice was strong.

“‘I shore thought some of you *big* boys would want to tag along with me, but now I see that y’all ain’t so brave after all. Well, I’ll just go by myself if there ain’t nobody goin’ with me.’ Etta Mae, as you can see, never let anybody get ahead of her. She went out on the porch with all the young'uns following to look in the direction of the graveyard, which was about a half a mile away.

"The moon was out, and they could see the outlines of the gravestones against the dark bushes. The wind had calmed down, but somehow somethin' seemed to be blowin' in the cemetery. As they strained to look into the dark night, they thought they could almost see yellow leaves from the scrub bushes flyin' around and around like a whirlwind was blowin' them. This was very strange. It was almost 10:30. Was this a sign?" Andrew Cockrell's voice had dropped to a whisper.

"Even the big boys on the porch were wild-eyed," Mr. Cockrell continued, "and some of the girls even turned around and rushed back into the house.

"Etta Mae was nervous but stubborn and determined. She said, 'I'm goin'. Anybody goin' with me?'

"Nobody said anything or moved. Etta Mae held her head a little higher, stepped off the porch, and started walkin' across the dark yard. One of the boys said, 'Hey, Etta Mae, how're we gone know if you've really been there? All you got to do is walk out of sight and then turn around and come back here and just say you went.' Etta Mae didn't even bother to answer.

"But then somebody thought of the idea of trimming off a stick, makin' it sharp so that it could be stuck in the ground, and tying a white flag or cloth or somethin' on it.

"'Wait up, Etta Mae,' said one of the boys. 'All you gotta do is take this sharp stick, go up there, jab the stick on one of them graves, turn around, and come back. Then in the morning we can go up there and see if that stick is sticking up on a grave. If it is, we'll know you've been there.'

"Etta Mae answered him, still smiling that smile. 'I agree to that.' She took the stick, started walking toward the graveyard in the dark, and disappeared clean out of sight."

Mr. Cockrell paused, got up from his chair, and went to the kitchen for a dipper of water. When he returned, he found the children arguing loudly about what happened to Etta Mae. As he sat back down, the children had an uneasy look on their faces. Questions began to fly. "Is that the end of the story? Did she come back to the party? Did she try to fool everybody and go back home? Was the stick in the grave? Did the ghost light get her?"

"If you young'uns'll give me a chance, I'll finish the story."

You can bet all the children fell silent. Mr. Cockrell cleared his throat, and this time his voice was softer than it had been before, which added to the fright of the tale. He continued.

"After Etta Mae left for the cemetery, all of the children went back in the house and began to play games again, but they just couldn't keep their minds on spin the bottle. Everybody began to eye the old clock on the mantelpiece. 'It's fifteen minutes to 11:00,' whispered one of the girls anxiously.

"Minutes passed, but every minute seemed like an hour. One of the younger boys couldn't stand it any longer. He started whining, 'Y'all know what? I bet that old clock done broke down.'

"'Naw it ain't. See the old pendulum's swingin' back and forwards. And you can still hear that *tick-tock* sound,' the other children told him.

"Everybody got real quiet. The wind began to blow again. They couldn't hear anything but the groanin' of the wind as it whipped around the house and the *tick-tock*ing of the clock. The minutes stretched out like that pull candy they were makin' in the kitchen. The children just couldn't hide their fear, fakin' a smile or pretendin' a yawn. Their only thought was of Etta Mae. Where was she? Why didn't she come back?"

Mr. Cockrell got up and stretched, sat back down, and continued.

"Suddenly the children heard loud laughter comin' from the dining room, even though the door was closed. 'I guess the grownups are having a real good time,' said one of the children.

"'Oh my lord. Etta Mae's ma and pa are back there havin' fun with all the rest of the grownups. They don't know about Etta Mae!' The children knew what they had to do.

"Everybody caught on real fast.

"'We should've told everybody about Etta Mae goin' to the graveyard. Every one of the grownups are gonna be mad, and Etta Mae's ma and pa are gonna be the maddest,' one of the girls said, and her voice was shakin' when she said it.

"Three of the big boys stood up, looked at each other for courage, and opened the door to the kitchen. One of the grownups laughed and boomed, 'What's the matter with you boys? Seen a ghost?'

"One of the boys blurted out, 'Yes, sir!' The other two yelled, 'No, sir!'

"The grownups saw that the boys were nervous, but they were real polite and waited for an explanation. Finally one of the boys cleared his throat and said, 'Etta Mae done went off to the graveyard about an hour ago right by herself, and she ain't come back.'

"Etta Mae's mother screamed, 'No! No! My little girl! What's happened to her!' The other women rushed to her side and tried to comfort her.

"Etta Mae's daddy was mad. His usual soft voice was gone. He yelled out, 'Everyone of you young'uns ought to be whipped.' Then his soft voice returned. 'I know, I know. You children meant to tell us. You just forgot. That Etta Mae was born stubborn.'

"One of the grownups said, 'We're wasting time. We've got to find her. You men run home and get your lanterns.'

"All of the men trooped out with a determined look on their faces, leavin' the women sitting around the table trying to comfort Etta Mae's ma. The last man out yelled to the others, 'Don't forget your lanterns.'

"The children stood on the porch in little groups waitin' for the men to return. Even though no one could hear them, they talked in whispers. The night was pitch dark. The only sound was the chirping of the crickets and the occasional hoot of an old owl.

"Finally one of the boys whispered, 'Look at all the lights bobbin' up and down.' The lights were the lanterns of the walkin' men comin' back from the graveyard. The crickets stopped chirpin', and even the old owl hoots got quiet.

"The men walked up, put their lanterns on the porch, and walked right by the children into the house without sayin' a word. Etta Mae wasn't with 'em. Everybody crowded around, expectin' the worst.

"One of the men stepped up on a footstool and in a tremblin' voice said, 'We found Etta Mae. She was lying next to a gravestone. A sharp stick was stickin' in the grave, but the stick also went through the back edge of her skirt. She likely turned to leave and thought somethin' had her. I guess she died of fright.'

"There wasn't a dry eye in the crowd."

Mr. Cockrell stood up, and all of us children thought the story was over. Mr. Cockrell suddenly said, "One more thing. Years passed, and the people in the neighborhood had different ideas on how Etta Mae died. Some agreed that she died of fright. Some said it was the ghost light that did it. And you know what? That ghost light hasn't paid another visit to that graveyard since. Not yet anyway." He grinned. "Good night, children. Sweet dreams."

Needless to say, I didn't have sweet dreams that night or for several nights. For years, even after I became a teenager, every time I passed a country graveyard, I thought of Etta Mae. However, when I became a father, it was my delight to pass this tale on to my boys. There's just something about a good, scary Halloween story!

CHAPTER TWELVE

It Takes a Neighborhood

MY GRANDFATHER, James Pharoah Cooper, was born on July 1, 1859, two years before the Civil War began. How he got the name Pharoah, I'll never know. Was he related to the early Egyptian kings? I don't think so. The spelling isn't exactly the same, although if you had asked me about it when I was a child, you would have gotten an affirmative answer.

Everybody called him Fed, except his twenty-one grandchildren and some of the neighborhood children, who called him Pa Fed.

Pa Fed was about six feet tall, as sturdy as an ox and hard as nails. He was rarely seen without his flat-brimmed black hat. His laugh was a little deep-throated chuckle, never loud or boisterous, but most of the time he had a grim look on his wrinkled face.

"You young'uns get down from that dogwood tree. You'll break the limbs. Stop throwing rocks at the chickens. You might hit one of the mules," he would yell to the ten or eleven grandchildren playing in the yard.

Sound like a mean old man? Not to me. I loved him, and I was absolutely certain that he loved me. Back in those days I took our relationship for granted and never thought about it, but now that I'm eighty years old, I am thinking about it. Why did Pa Fed and I have such a close relationship? Whenever I spent the night with my grandparents, I always slept with him, and I believe I was the only grandchild ever invited to share Pa Fed's bed. If he wanted to show someone the new nest he had constructed for his turkey hen, he could count on me to be interested. When I wanted to know how to keep sweet potatoes from freezing, he proudly explained his potato hill, made of dirt and straw piled up in a cone shape with the potatoes nestling in the center, protected from the frigid weather.

I guess we were close because I, being an only child, was accustomed to relating to adults one on one. Not only with my parents, but all the neighbors on the path.

First, there was Mr. Van, who always welcomed me, particularly in the summer at the tobacco barn. He was usually lying on his canvas cot reading about Australian Aborigines in a *National Geographic*, or immersed in his favorite magazine, *Stories of the Wild West*. I remember well the many entertaining afternoons Mr. Van spent reading aloud to me. "The Silver Kid, dressed in his black leather pants, rode slowly down Main Street, his black horse dripping with sweat which almost evaporated before hitting the dusty street. The snarling watch dog stationed under the saloon porch raised his head and with a muffled growl crawled halfway, looked up at the approaching visitor, then quickly surrendered to the blistering sun, sliding back into his spot of shade," he would read. I still like westerns, and *National Geographic* will always be my favorite magazine. Inspired, I'm sure, by those early conversations, as an adult I even spent a month rambling through the Australian outback, getting to see firsthand those Aborigines Mr. Van had told me about.

In addition, Mr. Van was a beekeeper. We would walk down to the edge of the woods where he kept his beehives, and I would ask a thousand questions about the care and feeding of bees. He enjoyed answering my questions, and I know I enjoyed listening. Later on, I kept bees myself.

A little farther down the path lived Uncle Bob and Aunt Addie, brother and sister. They had no children, so they considered me theirs, and I took advantage of that fact by eating at their trough whenever possible. Uncle Bob knew how to do many things, but growing trees was one of his main interests. He tried to teach me how to graft one type of apple tree to a different kind so that the grafted tree would bear two different types of apples. I never acquired that skill, but as a result of our many conversations, I was able to grow and sell some of the best peaches in the area.

No discussion of neighbors would be complete without my favorite Aunt Addie story. She was a hard worker, but she did a lot of sitting on the front porch. On one occasion when I walked up she had just finished scrubbing her porch and was preparing to rest a spell in her favorite rocking chair. Suddenly her Rhode Island Red rooster flew up on the porch, looked around, surveyed the scene, and decided to use the nice clean porch as his private toilet. The ensuing splat brought Aunt Addie swiftly to her feet and, with her broom swishing through the air, she yelled, "Hell that chicken to the bitch!" Obviously Aunt Addie really didn't know how to curse, but this outburst seemed to fit the occasion and has certainly given me many a chuckle over the years.

Uncle Brad, next on the path, caught snakes for fun. He put them in screen wire cages, which he carefully placed on the front porch in spite of the violent protests of Aunt Ethel, his wife. There were more snakes in those days, and sometimes he would find a copperhead dangling from a tree or a king snake running through the weeds. Invariably, in challenging me to grab a snake and put it in a cage, he would ask me, "You want to try this one?" Although I wasn't afraid of them, my answer never changed and I never caught a snake. I did find them fascinating though.

Uncle Brad was the only foxhunter I ever knew who had fox hounds and a saddle horse that would run with the dogs. The English countryside and its foxhunts had nothing on Uncle Brad. Although I didn't get to ride the horse, I learned a lot about hunting, trapping, and fishing just by listening to his stories.

But Uncle Brad wasn't the only adult in his family to influence me. His daughter, Virginia, was a schoolteacher who was always ready to discuss books with an inquisitive child. I filled the bill. She suggested that I read Daniel Defoe's *Robinson Crusoe*. It was the first book I remember reading. I was captivated, enthralled, spellbound from the very first chapter. Mother reminded me of a chicken hawk circling in the sky, watching over me and my homework, which had begun to suffer. She admonished me to "get up your lessons, and then you can read that library book," but she caught me a couple of times with my schoolbooks open, reading intently, only to find *Robinson Crusoe* tucked inside. I remember that book in detail to this day.

Virginia also introduced me to Rafael Sabatini. I read many of his novels and spent delightful hours discussing the stories with Virginia. In June 2004, I ordered and received one of his out-of-print books, *The Lion's Skin*, first published in 1911. I appreciate her for instilling in me my joy of reading.

Perhaps, since communicating with adults was something that came easy to me, Pa Fed knew I was interested in what he had to say. I was a good listener, and so was he. Come to think of it, I was quite a talker, but he would always listen. In other words, we communicated.

Never will I forget one particular night. Pa Fed and I were lying on a cot at the tobacco barn. It was a dark, quiet night. Even the crickets were taking a nap. As we lay on our backs, gazing up into the sky, it seemed as though a blanket of stars covered us.

"Pa Fed, did you know that all those stars up in the sky are worlds?" I asked.

He was quiet for a while. Finally he spoke. "Who told you that?"

"Virginia. She ought to know. She's a teacher."

"I reckon so," he replied.

We were both very quiet, looking up in the sky surrounding us.

"Did you see that?" Pa Fed asked, pointing upward.

"Where?"

"You missed it."

"What was it?"

"It was a falling star," Pa Fed said. We were both silent for a while. Pa Fed broke the silence and with a slight smile said, "You reckon that world was destroyed? You think there were any people on that world?"

It was my time to be silent. Finally I mumbled, "I hadn't thought of that."

You know, after thinking back on it, I don't think Pa Fed believed one word about all stars being worlds. He was right, of course. I had misunderstood Virginia's musing about some star somewhere being inhabited. But, being Pa Fed, he had just listened and gently corrected me. That's one of the many reasons I loved him.

Pa Fed died on May 2, 1940. I was thirteen years old. I still miss him.

CHAPTER THIRTEEN

Alone, but Never Lonely

ALL OF MY COUSINS were blessed with multiple siblings, as were my close friends. I was the only one in our group who had no brothers or sisters. My cousins Marvin Watson and Grover Cooper were only children, but Marvin was born much later, in 1945. Grover lived in Washington, D.C.

As far as I was concerned, my situation was unique, and I enjoyed my solitude. Inquisitive with a burning desire to know everything, I took advantage of every opportunity. How does a young country boy satisfy an insatiable appetite for learning? He doesn't entirely. I still have it.

In addition to the incredible input from my neighbors on the path, my parents gave me almost unlimited freedom to explore the world that surrounded me. Although no money was available for extras, they provided what they could and allowed my imagination to do the rest.

One day Daddy drove up in his old truck. As always, when he came from Nashville, I would run to meet him, expecting a brown paper sack with five one-cent pieces of candy. This time he handed me the sack, and as I turned to go, he said, "I brought you something else."

"Oh boy! More candy!"

"No. Look in the back of the truck. There's a pasteboard box."

I climbed up on the truck body, and sure enough there was a box. Taking a closer look, I saw little holes cut in the box. "Why are those little holes cut in the box?" I asked.

"So they can breathe."

With trembling hands, I lifted the lid and peeped in. "Ducks! Ducks!" I yelled with delight.

"I thought you'd like them. Now you have your chickens and your ducks to look after. Your ducks are half grown. One is a drake and the other two are hens. You'll have to keep them in a pen until they get used to their new home. Think you can do that?"

"Oh, yes, yes!" I cried out with anticipation and delight.

I put the ducks in a wire enclosure that had formerly been the garden. Their shiny, just turning black feathers glittered in the sunlight with the slick green head of the little drake towering above the rest. After about two weeks, however, I felt comfortable taking down the wire and letting them roam free with the chickens. They had quickly learned where their next meal was coming from!

The ducks, I discovered as the days went by, had habits not at all like my chickens. For example, they refused to lay eggs anywhere around the yard or in prepared nest boxes as the chickens did, and, as soon as they were granted freedom from the enclosure, they began to explore the woods. The soon-to-be mama duck would waddle across the pasture looking back at me to be sure she wasn't being followed. I would look the other way and feign indifference.

To protect her babies she needed complete secrecy and planned to cover her eggs with dirt and leaves, leaving no hint as to their location. The only way I could keep a check on her family was to follow her to the nest site in the woods before she laid her eggs. When she finally satisfied herself that I was not interested, she started the journey to her selected spot, laid her eggs, and carefully camouflaged them. Little did she know that I had followed like a police tail. I had a nest to watch until the yellow, and sometimes black, ducklings poked their heads out of the eggs to discover a new world. Finally they became strong enough to follow their mother to the yard. There the mother and her brood found the water hole I had already dug for them to play and swim in.

I soon learned that the baby ducks were far too young to eat the grains of corn I showered around the little pond. The adult ducks were walking around as if they were showing the little ones how to shovel up the corn with their flat bills, but every once in a while the mother duck would stop and crank her head to one side to gaze at her children futilely nibbling at the grains of corn. She seemed to say, "Not now. The grains are too big for you! But when you get a little older, corn will be one of your favorite foods."

That gave me an idea. Why not try corn meal? I did. The little ones crowded around a pan piled high with the fluffy, white corn meal I provided, pushing one another to secure a spot at the table, gobbling up the delicacy before them as if they were starving, while I kept the adults at bay.

One of my favorite pastimes had been watching the ducklings swim and splash in the pond I had dug for them. However, after my smashing success with the corn meal, whenever I walked into the yard, the little ones rushed between my legs and on top of my boots looking for more of that great white stuff. No more swimming around for them when the great provider put in an appearance. What to do?

After some meditation and serious problem solving, I hit upon an idea. Why not make a little pine bark boat, fill it with corn meal, and launch it on my duck pond? I'll bet they would quickly decide to take a dip.

I ran back of the chicken house where we kept wood for warmth and cooking. There I found a piece of pine bark that I easily whittled into something resembling a boat, filled it with meal, and launched it on its maiden voyage into the middle of the little pond. The babies took one look and dived in the water. With my body stretched so that one leg was on one side of the pond and the other leg on the other side, I watched them swimming around enjoying their evening meal. I don't know who was more delighted, the ducks or me!

Time was meaningless, and before I knew it the sun was hanging low over the pine trees in back of my house and the chickens were coming in the yard, headed for the henhouse for the night. When they saw the activity around me and all that duck food for easy picking, the chickens rushed over, jumped in my little duck pond, overturned my carefully filled pine bark boat, and kicked, stepped on, and shoved my sweet little ducklings. I was furious!

I jumped up and waved my arms to shoo away the intruders, but to no avail. In a rage, forgetting all my training, I found a tobacco stick propped against the chicken coop nearby, grabbed it, and, seething with anger, swung it in the midst of the flying chickens. Suddenly I felt a thud and froze. One of the young chickens was flapping up and down in its final death struggle. I looked with horror at the lifeless creature.

In life when things get really bad and we think they can't get worse, oftentimes they do. As I stood gazing at the horrible result of my tantrum, out of the corner of my eye I saw Daddy, who had worked late in the fields, walking rapidly up the path.

"I can hardly believe what I just saw you do!" Daddy shouted as he came up to me. "That chicken isn't even fryin' sized!" And with the hand that had never before touched me in anger, my daddy unceremoniously slapped me on the butt. Boy, did it hurt. Not my butt, my heart.

Daddy quickly turned and walked in the house. I was devastated. My heart was broken. I sat down on the chopping block at the woodpile, and the tears flowed. Mother soon appeared on the back porch and called me to supper, but I continued to sit on the block and sob.

Finally, Daddy opened the back door, looked at me with kindness, and gently said, "Come on in to supper, son."

I knew immediately that he was also sad. After all, it was a first time for him too.

I wish I could say that this incident taught me never again to lose my temper. Unfortunately, that is not the case, but you can rest easy in the knowledge that all my future outbursts were tempered by the memory of that unexpected, devastating slap on the butt.

Raising chickens and ducks wasn't the only way my parents encouraged me to explore my world and satisfy my curiosity. Things like honeybees, tadpoles, peach trees, and flowers taught me science, history, math, business, and psychology. But not all my projects could be labeled successful.

The Pond

IN THE WOODS behind my house a spring branch ran from one end of our farm to the other on its way to Sapony Creek. The water was as clear as the drinking water we drew from the well, and my winged aquatic friends certainly preferred the branch over the yard. Home to tadpoles, roaches, crayfish, frogs, and water moccasins, the branch was a favorite playground for a young country boy filled with curiosity.

One day, while sitting on the bank of the branch and thinking about how much my ducklings were enjoying the tiny pond I had provided for them in the yard, an exciting idea popped up in my brain. My ducklings would welcome with gusto a larger pond! And I knew just how to get it for them. "I'll build a private pond big enough for all my ducks to swim in and enjoy. Big enough to raise fish in so that I can fish and play right here behind my house!"

How do I build a pond that big? Simple, just construct a dam across the branch. The water will back up, and I'll name it Cooper's Duck and Fish Pond!

Immediately I began digging, shoveling, and throwing dirt and mud on the few rocks that I had placed strategically in the run of the branch. I worked for an hour or more, sweat rolling across my brow and into my eyes, muscles aching. Gradually the flow of water slowed, and my pond became deeper and deeper. Wiping the water from my eyes, I surveyed the scene and decided with relief that Cooper's Duck and Fish Pond was big enough. I threw down my shovel, wiped muddy hands on wet pants already streaked with dirt, and settled comfortably against a tree, smiling happily at my vision of happy ducks jumping into cool waters.

In a moment, however, I noticed something strange. Trickles of water were rapidly beginning to pour out of my pond on the other side of the dam. In a few minutes, to my despair, my wonderful dam broke; the pond emptied quickly, and the branch continued unrestrained on its merry way to Sapony Creek.

What did I learn this time? Well, dreams don't always come true, particularly when you need to review your construction plans.

Tadpoles

ONE DAY IN THE latter part of May just before school closed for our summer vacation, we were all headed home on the crowded school bus. I was seated between two high school boys who were angrily discussing a science test. "I never heard Mrs. Johnson even mention a tadpole. Did you?"

"Naw. Did you?"

"Naw. Well, come to think of it, maybe she did mention it when she was naming the creatures that live in the creeks and branches around here."

That got my attention. My failure to create a pond had not stymied my love for exploring the branch.

The boys continued. "Well, if she did, I never heard anything about a tadpole turning into a frog."

A girl sitting nearby joined in. "Yes, she did. She told us that a tadpole drops its tail and gills and becomes a frog."

The boys snickered. "Well, has anybody ever seen that happen?" they asked.

And that was the end of the conversation.

It was not the end for me. If tadpoles really change into frogs, I wanted to be there to see it. Although the branch was full of black tadpoles, some with legs, I had never seen one actually turn into a frog.

Every afternoon for many days I patiently watched tadpoles up and down the creek. Not a single one metamorphosed.

Finally Daddy asked me why I was spending so much time at the branch. "Well, Daddy, I was trying to see a tadpole turn into a frog. The science teacher said they would."

Daddy grinned, "Oh, that's what you've been doing." Then he proceeded to tell me that it takes a long time for that to happen. It's a slow process.

I quickly challenged his response. "But I should see it happen if I look long enough, shouldn't I?"

Daddy thought a minute, smiled, and then questioned me. "Son, have you grown any in the past year?"

"Yes, sir," I answered, wondering what kind of question that was supposed to be.

"You look at yourself in the mirror almost every day, don't you?"

"Yes, sir."

"Did you see yourself grow?"

"Well, no."

Daddy left, headed to the lot to catch the mule to go to the field. He always did that to me, leaving me with unanswered questions to figure out for myself.

And I never did see a tadpole turn into a frog, but life on the farm continued to be one exciting project after the other.

CHAPTER FOURTEEN

Peach Trees and Honeybees

THE INSPIRATION for one of my favorite and most lucrative projects came from an unlikely source: eighth-grade agriculture, a subject the other two musketeers, Allen and Roger, had to convince me to take. In 1941, with only eleven years of public school, eighth grade was the first year of high school.

"School's gonna be tough!" I remember Allen saying. "Math, chemistry, English, and history. We're gonna be up every night, burning the midnight oil. If we don't make good grades, not only will our teachers be on us, but just think what'll happen when we get home!" Allen shook his head, eyes clouded with anxiety.

Allen's message was clear. It was going to be a difficult nine months. As we exited the bus that had pulled up behind the old brick school building, all three of us began talking at once until Roger quietly said, "Heck. It'll be OK."

"Yeah, you can say that," Allen snapped. "You're so smart, you don't have to work on your lessons."

Roger didn't agree with that outburst, but it was true. Roger didn't have to study to get good grades like Allen and I did.

"I know what you mean," I sympathized with Allen. "I'm worried too. But what can we do about it?

"Well, it's my understanding that Mr. Powers, you know, they call him 'Shorty Powers,' teaches agriculture. Everybody says first year's a snap. One guy said you don't even have to read the book, and you can still make a good grade."

"Sounds good to me," agreed Roger.

"Not me! I'll never be a farmer, and I certainly don't need agriculture to go to college!" I declared, but then I remembered the three musketeers. We always stick together. "Oh all right," I grinned. "Ag I it is."

The first day we arrived in Mr. Powers's room, everybody was standing around in the back talking to each other. *Pretty casual*, I thought. I glanced around and saw in the front center of the room a big old reddish-brown desk backed by a blackboard reaching almost the entire width of the room. On it was written in huge letters "FFA." Colorful pictures were thumbtacked to bulletin boards on each side of the desk: a field of cotton, tobacco being loaded on a pickup truck, and a boy dressed in a beekeeper outfit, standing in the middle of a beautiful peach orchard, transferring what looked like honey from one of the hives. "What in the world does FFA mean?" I asked Roger.

"You oughta know that. Future Farmers of America."

After that explanation, I was sure that my hours in this class would be boring. But I was wrong. Mr. Powers was young and enthusiastic and, after hearing only a few of his lectures, I was hooked. I had been on a farm all my life and thought I knew everything there was to know about farming. But Mr. Powers opened my eyes.

He told us about growing peach trees, planting blackberries, and raising cattle or even honeybees. He showed me a whole new world of money-making home entertainment! When he explained that I would need bees to cross-pollinate the peach trees I had chosen for my class project, I was ecstatic. Hey, I could see myself, just like the guy in the picture on the bulletin board!

Not only did Mr. Powers lecture to us the full hour each day in the classroom, sometimes even keeping us overtime so that we would have to rush to get to the next class on time, but also to my amazement I found that his dedication extended beyond school hours. Discussing my project after class one day, he explained to me that in order to grow nice peaches the trees should be planted in a loam-based sandy soil. "On the southwest side of my house there's a sandy field. I think the sand's pretty deep," I told him.

"Sounds like a good place for your trees," he replied.

That afternoon when the school bus stopped at the mailbox at the end of the path, I jumped off and started walking briskly up the hill ditches, thinking about the sandy field beside my house and about loam-based soil, whatever in the world that was. At that moment two blasts from a horn caused the chickens to fly in every direction. I looked up, and there was Mr. Powers. "I'm coming to see this soil you've got beside your house to see if we can order those trees," he grinned at me.

Mr. Powers coming to my house? No teacher had ever been to my house before, except Miss Sallie Braswell. She came when I stuck a pocketknife in the fingernail I was cleaning when the radiator blew up in the room. I was confident, however, that Mr. Powers's visit would be much more pleasant.

After checking the soil and the location, Mr. Powers approved the site. Since it was a school project, Daddy somehow came up with the eight dollars needed to order twenty trees out of Mr. Powers's catalog. The three weeks it took for those trees to arrive seemed like three months. It was late October, a perfect time to set fruit trees.

Under the supervision of Mr. Powers, I measured the space between the trees: five rows with four trees in each row. We had just begun to dig our first hole when Daddy walked up with another pair of hole diggers and said, "Thought you might need some help." The ground was soft so it didn't take long to dig the twenty holes, add the proper fertilizer, and carefully place a peach tree in each hole.

For the next two years I watched and waited, watered and sprayed, and on Mr. Powers's advice carefully applied para di chlorobenzene to diseased tree roots. Finally my trees were in full bloom, ready to form their first fruit. "But you really need some bees," Mr. Powers told me. "You'll have peaches no matter what, but with bees to cross-pollinate, there'll be enough peaches for everybody in town."

Well, all right, I'll get bees, I told myself, *but where and how?* I thought we could figure out how to move the bees, but finding beehives was another matter. I asked everyone in the neighborhood and at school until finally a classmate, Hubbard Batchelor, stopped me in the hall with these welcome words: "Heard you needed some bees." Hubbard had three hives he was tired of messing with, he said, and I was welcome to them.

I could hardly wait to get home to tell Daddy that Hubbard had given me three beehives and all we had to do was go get them. "Is that all?" Daddy asked sarcastically. "And just how do we get these bees without getting stung?"

"Well, Hubbard said he'd plug up the holes to the hives as soon as the bees got in for the night. He thinks we ought to pick 'em up about 9:00 or 9:30 after the bees have a chance to get calm. Hubbard'll be waitin' for us."

Daddy somewhat reluctantly agreed. He suggested that we get a cotton sheet from the grading room to spread in the truck body so that when we placed the beehives in the body of the truck we could wrap them up with the cotton sheets. That would be an extra precaution in case the bees got restless. If any bees got out, they would at least be in the cotton sheet and not on us.

The hands of the clock finally drug around to 9:00 o'clock. We tied our pants legs tightly, and with those minimum preparations we headed out to Hubbard's. When we arrived at his house, we were happy to find that he had already plugged up the beehives so that the bees could not escape, or at least we hoped not. We carefully lifted the hives, which were sitting on an old bench behind the barns, placed them on the truck, wrapped them up in the sheet, thanked Hubbard, and drove carefully on our way.

At home Daddy steered the truck down in the middle of the peach orchard, and we prepared to unload the beehives. In the quiet of the night, the bees, no doubt irritated by riding over bumpy roads and up the hill ditches, sounded like millions of screaming, buzzing creatures trying to get out to sting their captors to death. Slowly unwrapping the sheet, we placed the buzzing hives on benches strategically positioned under the trees.

However, we decided to wait until the bees calmed down before pulling the plugs Hubbard had stuffed in the hives. Surprisingly that took only a few minutes. Finally, when the bee screams had transformed into a gentle hum, we quickly pulled the plugs and left, hoping the bees would make themselves at home.

Early the next morning, Daddy and I both sneaked out to my peach orchard to inspect our new tenants. To our delight they were going in and out of the hives and into the peach tree blossoms, making honey and peaches, all for sale. "I'm in the money now!" I boasted.

Soon I learned, however, that "in the money" was not necessarily easy money; it had to be earned. For example, in order to have nice peaches, free from worms, I had to keep the trees sprayed. Every other week was enough unless, of course, it rained. Now I knew that water was necessary for healthy crops, but every rain washed all the spray off my trees, and I had to do all that work all over again. And rain added to another problem: weeds. Keeping weeds out of the orchard was a tough job. To be honest, I found myself secretly praying for dry spells.

But some of the work was exciting. During that first summer I decided that I needed more bees to increase the already profitable production of honey. I figured it wouldn't be as much work as the peach orchard and might really be some easy money. I had the hives, but there was the same old problem: where could I get the bees? As a farm boy I worked outside just about every day of my life, and during the latter part of May I had noticed swarms of honeybees so big they would create a huge moving shadow beneath them. Fascinated, I would stop the mule and plow and gaze at them going overhead. Chester Yarborough, one of the men we had working for us, told me of a way to catch these honeybees if I was smart enough. I assume he meant I needed intelligence for the job.

"What you gotta do," he told me, "is keep a good lookout, and when you see a swarm comin', try to follow 'em as fast as you can to see which tree limb they light on if they light."

"When do they light?" I asked.

"Well, I don't know, but they got to stop sometimes," Chester explained patiently, "and when they do, just put your hive under 'em, throw some water on 'em, and they'll go right in the hive. I don't know 'bout that, but that's what my grandpa said."

Chester's instructions started me to thinking. Soon after that conversation, I was walking down the path behind my house when I saw the familiar dark cloud of bees heading my way. I craned my neck to see which way they were traveling, and, after determining their direction, I immediately began running across the field behind my house.

To my surprise they landed on a limb protruding from a sweet gum tree in the edge of the woods near the mule stable. There were so many bees on that limb that they hung down in the shape of a large cone, bending the limb almost to the breaking point. I immediately turned around and as fast as my legs would carry me I ran, grabbed an empty bee hive and a sheet and placed them on the ground beneath the bees.

Then I ran back to the well, drew some water, poured it in a bucket I found sitting on the wash bench, and retraced my steps at top speed. But I was not through. Next I retrieved a rope from the harness room, and, nearly out of breath by this time, made it back to the tree limb full of bees.

After catching my breath I carefully moved under the end of the limb, ran the rope through the branches of the limb, tied a knot, and slowly with the rope in my hand came back a good distance from the hive. To my surprise, most of the bees remained in their position in the cone, which left very few bees flying around.

Next I shook the limb as hard as I could. The bees fell on the cotton sheet I had placed under the hive. Quickly cupping both of my hands, I splashed water on the pile of bees, hardly noticing the few that were flying around my face and ears. Suddenly to my delight they went pouring into the beehive like water running into a hole.

I was a tired but elated child who had captured his first hive of bees. After this new addition, all went well, and my business prospered. Keeping bees and a peach orchard was hard work for a teenager, but the money and praise plus my new understanding of the world around me made it all worthwhile.

Mother and Daddy arrive for
Big Daddy's Thanksgiving dinner.

CHAPTER FIFTEEN

Big Daddy Clark

When I was thirteen years old, Mother's father, Will Clark—or Big Daddy, as I called him—gave her twenty shares of Reynolds Tobacco stock "to help protect your future," he told her. Then he took the time to show me how to follow the progress of that stock each day in the newspaper the mailman slid in our box at the end of the path.

I was fascinated. What a life-changing thought! Money can do the work and make more money for me! From that moment I opened my own imaginary stock portfolio, pretend to be sure, but exciting nonetheless. After my research, which was severely limited, I would "buy" a thousand shares of a stock. When it went up, I would sell. When it went down, sometimes I would hold, hoping it would go up. If not, I would sell and reinvest in a different stock. I was a "millionaire" at the age of fifteen!

A good market brought me almost as much joy then as it does now, even though the money now is real. And I tried then, as I do now, not to be despondent over bad choices. Since Big Daddy's gift to my mother, I have never been without a stock portfolio. That unselfish gesture and valuable instruction probably changed my life. He was like that, changing lives and taking charge of events wherever he went.

My grandfather, whose full name was Will Elam Clark, was born in 1878, in Texas. It never occurred to me to wonder about Big Daddy Clark's background until my later years when my mother was ninety years old. She was confused as one gets at that age, but when I questioned her about Big Daddy Clark's origins she answered promptly: "One day he just got off the train in Rocky Mount, coming all the way from Texas. He came to Nashville and got a job with old man Askew Batchelor. Askew was rich and owned a lot of property and a saw mill, you know."

That bit of information whetted my appetite, and I wanted to know more about this man who was so important in our lives. One of my cousins, Fenner Clark, had the same idea and did quite a bit of research, which his mother Cora and sister Sara were kind enough to share with me.

But it wasn't until my cousin, Winkie Bell, moved to Texas that we learned that Will's father, our great-grandfather Junius Clark, was a surveyor for the railroad and worked on the construction of a railway headed south from Richmond and hurriedly built for use in the Civil War. Apparently Junius kept going because he and his family ended up in Texas, where he was buried. I was pleased to find that Mother's information about Big Daddy getting off a train from Texas was no doubt correct.

As Mother had indicated, Mr. Askew Batchelor, obviously a learned man, quickly recognized that young Will was intelligent and dependable. He gave Will more and more responsibility, finally making him general manager of all the Batchelor operations. Having Will Clark in charge made it possible for Mr. Batchelor to retire soon thereafter, and Big Daddy became one of the most important men in the area.

It appeared, however, as if Big Daddy's mind was not always on business. A young lady named Natolia Nobles, but called Toley, who lived four miles west of Nashville, caught his eye, and the story goes that Miss Toley was more than willing to accept his attention. Soon thereafter, Big Daddy asked Miss Toley's father for her hand in marriage. At first Mr. Nobles agreed to the match, but later, to the young people's shock, he changed his mind and refused to give his permission. Faced with this dilemma, the young lovers carefully planned their elopement.

Somehow Mr. Nobles learned of their plan and appeared just as Big Daddy drove up in his buggy to fetch his bride-to-be. Not to be deterred, Toley threw her suitcase in the buggy and jumped in. But to their dismay, her father, whose buggy was nearby, gave chase as they rode off. The story goes that some of the neighbors saw two buggies fly past, in a cloud of dust, the horses wildly responding to the lashing buggy whips.

Evidently Big Daddy won the race. They were married. Toley was nineteen years old at the time. My mother was born not long after, in 1903, but joy soon turned to tragedy. One morning, someone (perhaps Big Daddy) found my three-month-old mother crying by the body of his beloved Toley, and Big Daddy had to draw on his great reserve of strength to begin life all over again. He immediately placed my mother, his baby girl, in the home of his sister, Ola Clark Overby, who cared for her as if she were her own daughter.

Fifteen years later, Big Daddy married Annie Rackley. My mother told me that when Big Daddy came to take her to his newly established home she was so sad and upset she hid behind the piano, trying to avoid the inevitable. Aunt Ola had been the only mother she had ever known, and leaving her was another wrenching blow. As Uncle Tom, Toley's brother, told me many times, my mother had a hard life, but she continued the relationship with Aunt Ola as best she could. When I was a young child, Mother and I visited Aunt Ola and her husband Uncle Bill in Rocky Mount as often as possible. Aunt Ola died in 1933.

Big Daddy and Annie had three children: one daughter, Louise, and two sons, Wayland Earl (we called him Pete) and Bill Fenner (we called him Billy). Mother always said she felt like a mother to her younger sister and brothers.

The Clark property grew over the years, in spite of a huge fire that destroyed his general merchandising store and all of his other buildings on the block. Big Daddy eventually located his family on about forty acres on Business Highway 64 east of Nashville, establishing a new store near the road and building a pond with ducks and geese where everyone could enjoy fishing.

Clark's store was a meeting place for anyone who knew Will Clark and for people he didn't know because Will Clark never met a stranger. He was a big man with a commanding presence. If you were anywhere nearby, you were invited any day of the week to the house for lunch, for conversation, or for whatever else was going on. But holidays were special, and Christmas was the most celebrated holiday of all, a four-day event.

On the back porch, there was a long table that would seat about ten people. Other, smaller tables placed strategically around the house made it possible to feed any number of people, and when we had pretty weather, guests would even find spots under the pine trees. On holidays the crowds ate in shifts, doubling or tripling the number served.

How Mama Clark accomplished this feat I will never understand

Even though there were always several ladies who volunteered to help in the kitchen, Mama Clark was the one who was responsible for everything. She always prepared crispy fried chicken, succulent slabs of country ham, aromatic young turkey and dressing, and, at Big Daddy's special command, a roasted, grinning possum, at the center of the table. It had been especially fed and fattened in a straw-filled barrel before the holidays just for the occasion. It was not my favorite dish. In fact, I even defied Big Daddy by refusing to follow his bellowed instructions to "Eat it! Taste it! It's good!"

Big Daddy had an interesting rule, that the bowls of steaming corn and potatoes and green beans and peas must always be full, even at the end of the meal! I guess he wanted everyone to have, as they say, "a plenty."

One year, for some reason, Big Daddy decided to have an early Thanksgiving meal with just the family, and the preacher as the only guest. It had to be early because the crowds would pour into the house Thanksgiving Day.

Big Daddy wasn't much of a drinker, but he did like a little toddy before his meal. Before that particular Thanksgiving meal, the women in the kitchen discussed the matter. "What are we going to do about Will taking a toddy right in front of the preacher?"

Mother had an idea. "Mama," she suggested, "why don't you just ask Papa not to take a drink today with the preacher here?"

"You know how Will is, but I'll try," Mama Clark said, wiping her hands on her apron and moving quickly to the back porch where Big Daddy was sprawled on the sofa enjoying his grandchildren, me included. "Will," her voice was strong but pleading, "the preacher'll be here in a minute. Please don't take a drink before dinner with him here."

Big Daddy's eyes opened with surprise. "Why not?" he demanded.

"Because it's wrong," Mama Clark explained.

"What's wrong with it?"

"Because it's a sin, Will."

"You really think it's a sin?"

My mother, overhearing the conversation, joined them on the porch. "Yes, I agree. It is a sin, Papa."

"Well, I tell you what," Big Daddy answered, "when the preacher gets here, I'll ask him what he thinks about it."

I had followed this conversation with interest. When Big Daddy made what to him must have seemed a perfectly logical suggestion, I thought Mother and Mama Clark were going to faint on the spot. "Oh no, please don't do that!" they begged.

I watched with interest the arrival of the preacher, waited with the men at the dinner table, and listened carefully to Big Daddy's conversation. Soon he leaned back in his chair and said, "Preacher, I usually have a little dram before dinner. Would you care to join me?"

"No, thank you, Mr. Clark," the preacher responded.

"Well, would you mind if I do?"

"No, go right ahead."

Well, at least Big Daddy adhered to part of Mama Clark's and Mother's plea. He didn't ask the preacher if he thought drinking was a sin, but he did take a drink. As you have no doubt gathered, Will Clark didn't ask; he told. That was a Thanksgiving dinner I'll never forget.

Everybody loved Big Daddy and buzzed around him like workers to the queen bee, but he had a habit that I'm not sure was always appreciated. He visited his friends whenever it suited him, even early in the morning before anyone in the household was awake. I distinctly remember one such morning. None of us were up when we heard the blast of a horn and a deep voice booming, "Get up! Get up! Time to get up! Thought you were farmers."

I was sleeping in my bed next to Mother and Daddy, but with the squeaking of the bedsprings, Daddy's feet hitting the floor, and Mother mumbling "Oh no," my eyes opened. Daddy, struggling to put on his bib overalls, glanced at the old clock on the mantelpiece and whispered hoarsely, "It's quarter to four! When does he sleep?"

Well, one thing was clear. There was no more sleep for me with Big Daddy around, so I bounded out of bed. Mother went straight to the kitchen as usual, and Daddy and I went out on the front porch. Big Daddy was sitting in his truck, his broad shoulders nearly filling the truck cab. When he saw Daddy and me, he turned his body toward us and planted his feet on the running board. "Haven't seen y'all in two or three weeks. How're your crops coming along?" he asked.

"We need rain," Daddy answered.

"No need to worry about that," Big Daddy assured him.

Mother joined us. "Won't you come in and have some breakfast, Papa?"

"No, Lois, Annie'll have breakfast for me when I get home. Just came by to see how y'all were doing and to talk to Roy about Tuesday's election. You know Harold Cooley has been our congressman for the last three years since Edward Pou died. Now he's got to run for election, and I want to help him all I can. He's depending on me to get him some votes. He's promised to help the farmers, and I know he will."

Will Clark had friends all over Nash County. Harold Cooley, an excellent politician, knew that. He was, in fact, elected for sixteen congressional terms and served Nash County well until his defeat by Republican Jim Gardner in 1966.

"I'll be glad to help you all I can," Daddy assured him. "I've got a lot of plowing to do, but I certainly intend to take time out to vote."

"How about you, Ditcher? Are you gonna help, too?" Ditcher was another of my nicknames, used only by Big Daddy. Mother called me Tommy because she thought I was another Tom Sawyer, but I never knew how Big Daddy came up with Ditcher.

"Sure," I responded enthusiastically, "but what can I do? I'm not old enough to vote!"

Big Daddy laughed. "But you got the right attitude, boy."

At about 4:30 in the afternoon of Election Day, Daddy was still working when lo and behold Big Daddy drove up a little path to the backfield where Daddy was plowing. He stopped his truck, rolled down the glass, and started talking before Daddy got to the end of the row. He hollered, "Thought you said you were gonna come and vote!"

"Well, Mr. Clark, it's only 4:30 in the afternoon, and the polls don't close until 6:00."

At that Big Daddy lowered his voice. "Well, Roy, I wanted to make sure you came. Why don't you just tie your mule to that tree at the end of the row, and I'll rush you on out there, and you can vote and I'll bring you back."

Wiping his hands on his dirt-streaked overalls, Daddy protested, "But I need to dress!"

"Dress? No you don't!"

Daddy looked down at himself, reluctantly agreed to climb in the truck, and off they went. Daddy voted that day along with many others Big Daddy either carried or urged to the polls.

Yes, Big Daddy Clark was a force in my life. Big Daddy was a force in any life he touched. He was an early inspiration for my political involvement later in life. He also taught me the importance of being a community leader. I am privileged to be his grandson.

CHAPTER SIXTEEN

Just a Little Dram

My uncle Tom was a kind, soft-spoken old gentleman. He was almost six feet tall, very slender, and always had what appeared to be a two-week-old, stubbly gray beard. Inevitably he had something nice to say to everyone and always had a grin on his face. After I describe his lifestyle, you may guess why he always had that grin.

It was almost dinnertime, and I was standing on the front porch. Mother was in the kitchen, bustling from one steaming pot to the other and checking on fluffy biscuits slowly browning in the oven. I just happened to look up toward Mr. Van's house and saw Uncle Tom walking very slowly past it. I reasoned that his slow pace was due to the fact that he had just conquered the hill ditches. I jumped off the porch and ran to meet him.

Uncle Tom would drop in every once in a while to see "Lo-wis" as he called my mother in a drawl, and when he came by he was always a little tipsy. Mother, being a good churchgoing Christian, a solid pillar in the Elm Grove Baptist Church located in our community, was against gambling, including any card game, cursing, and of course alcohol in any form. As you can imagine, Uncle Tom's nipping did not set well with her.

Uncle Tom walked up on the porch and called out, "Lo-wis, where are you? I know wherever you are, you're working. I know you and Roy are working too hard. You always are."

Uncle Tom was right. Mother was always working, and so was my daddy. They were a good pair.

Mother answered from the kitchen, "Here I am, Uncle Tom. You're right, there's always something that needs doin'. Come on in. Dinner'll be ready in a little while."

Uncle Tom opened the screen door, waved his arm around to shoo the flies away so that he could go in without letting the flies in with him to share dinner. "Lo-wis, I didn't come for dinner. I ate a late breakfast, and I'm not hungry."

"You always say that. Go on out to the back porch and wash your hands. The water bucket, pan, and soap are on the table. I see Roy down at the stables, turning the mules in the lot. He'll be hungry and will want to eat as soon as he comes in."

"Now, Lo-wis, I said I ain't hungry."

"I heard what you said. Go on and wash your hands and get ready for dinner. I've already set a place for you." Mother sniffed once, pursed her lips, and shook her head. My mother could detect the smell of alcohol a mile away, and you can be sure Uncle Tom would not escape her frown of frustration.

Daddy came in the back door. There wasn't a single dry thread in his overalls and shirt. He immediately headed for the water bucket, where he consumed at least three dippers of water, grabbed the towel from the rack, and wiped his face. Then, turning to face Tom who had just finished washing his hands, he grinned, extended his hand, and said, "It's good to see you, Tom. Did you come to help me finish plowing the cotton?"

Uncle Tom said with a grin, "I shore did. I think I could work a mule down."

About that time, Mother came out bringing another towel. "Roy, you did it again. You wiped your face before you washed it. Here."

Daddy, still smiling, looked at Tom. "She's always on me about keeping clean." Then Daddy turned and with a twinkle in his eye said to Mother, "Tom has agreed to help me finish plowing the cotton."

Mother answered, "I'm sure he thinks he can. He wouldn't last five minutes out there in that hot sun. He's been drinking again."

"Lo-wis, I just had one little dram."

"Tom, when you first came in I noticed that one of your pockets was bulged out, and it still is. Show us what you got in that pocket."

"Now, Lo-wis. All right." Uncle Tom reached in his pocket and pushing, pulling, and fumbling, he finally pulled out a flat, half-pint bottle of whiskey labeled Old Mister Boston. It looked like it was about half full.

Mother would invariably chastise Uncle Tom whenever he came around with that "whiskey smell," as she called it. I remember he had that "whiskey smell" every time he came to visit. Daddy was known to indulge once or twice a year, and he always said Mother had a bloodhound nose.

On this visit Mother had all the evidence she needed: the smell, the hidden bottle, and the most damaging evidence, the admission by Uncle Tom that he had had a "little dram." So Uncle Tom, faced with this overwhelming evidence, began arguing as he always did that it was perfectly all right to take a little drink. Knowing that Mother had an absolute belief in every word of the Bible, he had his defense all lined up.

"Lo-wis, did you know the Bible tells us in Timothy 5:23 to stop drinking nothing but water. It says, 'Drink no longer water, but use a little wine for thy stomach's sake and thine often infirmities.' Lo-wis, hit's right there in the Bible."

Mother came back with "Well, in your Bible reading I suppose you skipped over Proverbs, Chapter 20, Verse 1, which says that drinking too much makes you loud and foolish, that it's stupid to get drunk. And in Isaiah it says you're doomed if you get up early in the morning, start drinking, and spend long evenings gettin' drunk!"

Uncle Tom countered quickly. "But Solomon says, 'I have drunk my wine with my milk: eat, O friends; drink, yea, drink abundantly. . . .'"

The Bible quotes went back and forth like this for several minutes. I was amazed at Uncle Tom's knowledge of the Bible. I smile when I think about how Mother responded when I asked her about this later. "He does read the Bible a lot; it's a shame he doesn't get much out of it," she said.

After dinner, Daddy went back to continue plowing in the cotton field, which was located a good distance from the house. Uncle Tom lay down on the front porch and was snoring in short order. About two o'clock in the afternoon I went to the well to draw a bucket of water to take to Daddy in the field. Evidently the squeaking noise of the turning tickle wheel and the rattle of the chain and bucket woke Uncle Tom. He ambled up to the well. "I wanna drink of cool water, Tommy," he said, at the same time reaching for the gourd hanging from a nail on the side of the well. After he had drunk his fill, I began to pour water from the well bucket into a half-gallon jar.

"Gonna take water to Roy in the field, are you? Well, I think I'll tag along. I need the walk."

"Good." I always liked to talk to Uncle Tom when no one else was around.

We began our journey down the path, through the woods, and across the branch to the back field. This was a good chance for me to ask a question I'd wondered about for a long time. "Uncle Tom, why do you and Mother fuss every time you come to our house?"

"Well, Boy." (He called me "Boy" whenever we had a serious talk. Why, I don't know.) "Your ma always fusses every time I come 'cause she hates to see me when I'm a little tipsy. Now, Boy, I want you to promise me that you will never tell her about this little talk we're havin'."

"I promise." My feet shuffled in the dirt as we made our way down the path.

"Well, I just enjoy her always after me about nippin' and especially when she starts tellin' me it's a sin. You'll notice I'm always first to bring up the parts of the Bible that show it's all right to take a little nip. That makes her mad and she starts using Bible quotin' just like me. I don't have anybody else to argue with me 'ceptin' her. I really think it's all right to take a little drink if you can handle your strong drink. I can handle it. I never hurt anybody. I've never been in any trouble, and I never get drunk."

My eyes widened with disbelief. "Now, Uncle Tom, I've seen you when…"

"Well, now, Boy," he hastened to explain. "Hardly ever. And even then I don't bother anybody. Now, Boy, gettin' right down to answer your question about me and your ma fussin' whenever I come to see y'all, well, I reckon it's 'cause I know she cares about me. Really I ain't got nobody else that cares like she does. You know, of course, your ma is my sister's child and that she died when your ma was three months old. Your ma had to struggle every step of her life until she met Roy. Your ma's life has been kind of like mine. I wonder if Lo-wis knows how much I care about her."

I couldn't think of a thing to say, but in my heart there was a fervent prayer: "I hope to the good Lord she does."

We had reached the branch and carefully made our way across a narrow plank that served as a bridge.

"Now, Boy, I want to get somethin' straight with you. You should never start to messin' with liquor, wine, or beer or any kind of strong drink. Look at what it's done to me. I ain't healthy. I'm a lot younger than I look." Confession was difficult for Uncle Tom, but he bravely continued. "Now remember your promise. Don't you ever tell your ma or anybody else I said this. It's probably a sin to nip. I know it is if you can't handle it. So, my advice to you is never, never touch the stuff. It's catchin'."

My disbelief became astonishment. In a private conversation with me, Uncle Tom had done an about-face on the issue of drinking. He felt like he had said enough, I guess, and we silently continued on our way to the field to find Daddy standing with his mule and plow in the middle of a row waiting for his cool water.

Well, I kept my promise. I never told Mother of our little talk, but I prayed a lot, asking the Lord somehow to let Mother know that Uncle Tom had secretly agreed with her, and I really believe the Lord did just that.

CHAPTER SEVENTEEN

The Heavy Wagon

THE LONG, hot summer day was ending. The sun was beginning to cast long shadows as it slowly sank behind the woods, surrendering its hot rays. With the retreating sun, the rain showers in the late afternoon, and a gentle breeze, I could not have hoped for a more pleasant evening. Even the lightning bugs seemed to be celebrating by flashing their dim lights across the field in front of the porch. Smoke from two old buckets stuffed with burning rags to keep the mosquitoes at bay had a pungent, but pleasant smell. Plates and cups were softly rattling in the kitchen as Mother went about her never-ending job of washing dishes.

We had finished supper. Daddy was slowly rocking on the front porch in his favorite chair, and I was sitting on the front porch steps. Neither of us spoke, content to hear the whippoorwills whistling their favorite sing-song tune: *whippoorwill, whippoorwill, whippoorwill.*

To my pleasant surprise, Daddy, who was inclined not to talk very much, said, "This evening reminds me of the evening Papa told me a pretty good story about the Brinkley Hill and two men on a wagon. Want to hear it?"

Most of Daddy's private conversations with me were about my need for a college education, so when he offered to tell me a story about the eerie Brinkley Hill, you can bet I responded with an enthusiastic "Yes!"

Daddy began. "To the best of my recollection, Papa told it this way." And here is what I remember about the story:

Jeff Henderson and Sam Collie, who lived next door to each other, often drove their two-horse wagons to Nashville to get supplies. I can't for the life of me figure out why people called them two-horse wagons when they were always pulled by mules, but that's what they called them. Sam and Jeff took turns: one time Sam would drive his mules and wagon, and on the next trip Jeff would take his mules and wagon. Both of them were especially proud of their mules, and they were always arguing about whose mules were the strongest. Of course, everybody in the neighborhood thought all four mules were the strongest and best trained in the area.

As the story goes, on one of their trips to Nashville, it was Sam's time to drive. As usual, he drove down the dusty, rutted Main Street, turned to the hitching post in front of the general store, and tied the mules. A few men were sitting on the boardwalk in front of the store; Sam walked over and joined them. Jeff walked across the street to Nash Bar, located on the east side of where the courthouse is now.

After a couple of drinks of what Jeff called "rotgut whiskey," he went back to the general store. "Let's hurry and get out of here, Sam. It's almost night, and I sure don't want to go up the Brinkley Hill after dark."

Over the years, since Brinkley Gandy sold Marcum Cooper five hundred acres on the south side of Sapony Creek in 1785, folks had started calling the steep hill that rose just beyond the plank bridge over Little Sapony Creek the Brinkley Hill. Some mighty scary stories had circulated about it, including tales of ghosts and unexplained sightings. Some folks like Jeff avoided the Brinkley Hill at night, but Sam wasn't too worried.

"Oh, I wouldn't fret too much if I was you," Sam smiled. "I don't think we'll run into any ghosts."

He and Jeff quickly loaded their supplies and began the journey home. They followed the path that is today Old Bailey Highway, the same path where the Brinkley Hill is located. They had made a late start from home, and the sun was already down. Sam, handing the old lantern to Jeff, said with a chuckle, "Jeff, light the lantern and hang it on that hook next to the mules. Ain't nobody gonna run into us, but at least a little light'll make you feel better. Maybe the lantern will keep the ghosts away."

With the lit lantern hung, Jeff joined Sam on the wagon seat, which was nothing but a board nailed down on both sides of the wagon. Two people could sit on the board and place their feet on the floor to give them balance, which helped if one of the wagon wheels hit a bump or a hole.

Sam and Jeff rode in silence for a few minutes, then the mules began to trot. The summer had been so hot and dry that the two-track path had cracked the ground in places. Nothing could be heard but the *clap, clap, clap* of the mules' feet on the hard ground, the trace chains jingling, and the rumble of the wagon.

"What's the matter with them mules?" Jeff asked, his eyes darting from one side of the path to the other. "Our butts is gonna be bruised when we get home if we don't slow them mules down," he warned.

"You know these mules are always in a hurry when they're headin' home. They have to be reined in just like I'm doin' now," Sam explained.

"Mine don't. I can speak to them in a quiet, gentle voice, and they slow down without me even touchin' the reins."

"There you go again sayin' your mules is better than mine. Next thing you'll be claimin' they draw their own water at the well."

"All right! All right! End of argument," Jeff sighed, "but I think somethin's spookin' them mules." Jeff peered into the dark woods on each side of the wagon.

Still reining in the mules, Sam kept on. They had passed only four small houses and were pulling up beside the little one-room Elm Grove Church situated just a short distance from Sapony Creek bridge.

Suddenly the mules stopped, heads up and ears back. They were looking straight down the road toward the creek.

"What in the world!" Jeff exclaimed. "I told you! Oh lordy, I bet them mules seen somethin' or heard something. We're gettin' close to the Brinkley Hill. You know, Sam, people been talkin' for years about the Brinkley Hill being haunted, and I'll have to tell you, every time I have to come by here at night I'm always a-dreadin' of it."

"Now, Jeff, you don't believe them stories, do ya, about ghosts and goblins and all that mess?"

Jeff's voice trembled a bit when he answered, "Well, I don't know. I reckon I don't believe in haints [our word for haunts or ghosts], but still, I heard some folks that I know is honest talk about haints around Sapony Creek and the Brinkley Hill."

Sam settled the mules down, and they continued past the church and around the curve, close to the creek. All of a sudden the mules stopped dead still, heads held high. Total silence surrounded them for a few seconds, and then they heard a sound like a rainstorm coming straight at them. Wind swirled around the wagon. Leaves flew by, striking Sam and Jeff like hornets. The mules whinnied and stood up in their traces on their hind legs, Sam holding tightly to the reins. Suddenly the wind stopped still and the silence returned. It had been like a tornado in the middle of the calm. Sam jumped off the wagon, ran around to the mules. "Whoa, whoa!" He rubbed their quivering necks, getting them under control.

"What was that? Ain't no clouds. Look at them stars. Ain't a drop of rain fell. I tell you, I don't like it," Jeff whispered hoarsely.

"Well, it could have been a whirlwind," Sam mused, climbing back on the wagon, doubt and fear creasing his forehead. He clucked to the mules, at the same time tapping them with the reins. The mules still held their heads high, looking one way and then the other. Finally they obeyed the signal and started across the creek.

Just as the back wheels of the wagon rattled off the wooden plank bridge, a shrill, half-human growl came from somewhere down the creek. There was a stunned silence. The frogs stopped croaking. The July flies and crickets stopped their chatter. The white faces of Sam and Jeff gleamed pale in the darkness. The mules went wild. Sam had his hands full, trying to keep them from running away.

"What was that?" Jeff yelled. "It's gotta be them haints we've been hearing about!"

Sam, nearly out of breath after quieting the mules, said, "Well, it sounded kinda like a bobcat."

Jeff yelled back, "What you mean 'kinda like'? It sounded like a human to me or a haint! Let's get on up the Brinkley Hill, and I mean fast, too."

"Jeff, you and me finally agree on somethin'," Sam yelled, "Git up!" at the same time slapping the mules with the reins. The mules snorted, bent their heads low, thrust their bodies into their harnesses, dug their hooves into the hard, dry ground, and pulled. But the wagon refused to move one inch. "What the...," Sam exclaimed. "Why won't the wagon move? These mules are strong! Somethin' must be wrong with the back wagon wheels. They must be stuck! Jeff, go back there and see what's wrong."

Jeff got the lantern and began to crawl to the back of the wagon, slowly raising the light to get a better look. He suddenly turned pale with fear, dropped the lantern, and opened his mouth to yell, but nothing came out. Finally he half-stumbled, half-crawled back to his wagon seat.

Sam, still struggling with the mules, yelled out, "Jeff, we still ain't moving. What in tarnation's wrong?"

Jeff blurted out, "Somethin' black's on the back of the wagon. Somethin' black!"

Sam's voice was sharp and angry. "What?"

All Jeff could say was "Somethin' black, somethin' black. On the back of the wagon!"

"Well, gimme the lantern!" Sam reached with one hand, still holding the reins with the other.

"Hit's gone. The lantern's gone," was Jeff's feeble answer.

"Gone where?" Sam almost screamed.

"I dropped it when I saw what I seen," Jeff sobbed.

While all this was going on, the mules were still pulling, jerking, and pawing so hard that one of the mules fell down and was struggling to get up.

Sam threw the reins to Jeff. "Hold the mules then and let me go look."

Sam felt his way along the edge of the wagon until he got near the back. This time it was Sam whose eyes bulged and mouth went dry. Sure enough, the black thing was sitting on the back of the wagon. Sam, scrambling back to the front, croaked, "I believe you wuz right all along. A haint done got us."

Suddenly the mules fell forward as if a heavy load had been lifted, as if the wagon was empty. Jeff and Sam looked back. The black thing had disappeared.

The mules were running away, up the Brinkley Hill, but not fast enough for Sam and Jeff.

When Jeff and Sam got home, they told the neighbors what had happened, but some of them didn't believe the story. In the morning they went down to the bottom of the Brinkley Hill to see if they could find any signs of what went on. Sure enough they found where the mules had torn the ground up with hoof marks. Deep wagon tracks gouged in the rock-hard ground showed where the wagon had stuck at the bottom of the Brinkley Hill.

"Some of the neighbors were convinced, and some didn't believe a word of the story." Daddy smiled at me with a slow grin when he was finished. "How about you, son? What do you think?"

"What I want to know is what did the black thing look like? What was it?" I asked.

"Well, that's for you to decide. I've told you all I know. I do know that the heavy wagon story got added to the legends of the Brinkley Hill." Daddy resumed his rocking, and I knew more questions were useless.

I decided all right. I'd never let night catch me alone on the Brinkley Hill. Little did I know that my time would soon come.

CHAPTER EIGHTEEN

My Encounter with Brinkley Hill

MR. JOHNNY COOPER, who lived down the road from Pa Fed, had just finished putting in his last barn of tobacco for the year. He and his helpers, who included Dewey Lee and me, were in a festive mood. Mr. Johnny had a pig slowly barbecuing over the coals and iced tea sitting on the table.

Dewey Lee and I had been talking all day about going to Nashville to see a movie at the new Myers Theatre. We didn't know what was on, but we didn't care. Of course, during my day, parents didn't have to worry about whether a movie had an R rating. The thirty-five cents Mr. Johnny had just paid us was burning a hole in our pockets, as they say. We didn't have a care in the world except that school finally started Monday, a week later than scheduled, to give the school kids time to help finish putting in the summer's bumper crop of tobacco. Back then, the start of the public school calendar in Nash County was determined by farmers who needed their children to help harvest the crops.

Dewey Lee said, "It's already four o'clock." We ignored the barbecue, grabbed a welcomed glass of iced tea, gulped it down, and started at a slow trot to Dewey Lee's house. "You know it gets dark early somewhere around seven-thirty," he said. "We shore want to get back up the Brinkley Hill and home before it gets dark. Let's hurry and get to my house so we can get this tobacco gum off our hands." That gum is a sticky brown mess that collects on your hands when you're working with green tobacco.

After scrubbing and scraping our hands almost raw we were clean and ready to take off. Dewey Lee grabbed his bicycle and yelled out, "Let's go!"

All of a sudden I froze. "Dewey Lee, I left my bicycle at Pa Fed's. I'll have to go get it."

"No. We don't have time for that. Hop on my bike. We can go just about as fast 'cause when I get tired of pedaling we can stop and trade places and you can pedal. Come on."

I jumped on the crossbar, or side saddle as we called it, and we were off.

As you can imagine, two people riding on one bicycle on a dirt road is more difficult than it is on a hard surface road, but as long as you rode in the narrow wheel tracks where the dirt had become hard by the continuing passage of the automobiles, you were OK—that is, until you encountered the sandy spots. That's when things got tougher.

When we got to the Brinkley Hill, we coasted down fast. It wasn't so bad in the daylight. We were on our way, but not before we cast a nervous look back up the Brinkley Hill. I whispered, "See you later, Mr. Brinkley Hill, but it'll be before dark." I didn't know that Dewey Lee heard until he agreed with an "Amen!"

Dewey Lee was right when he said we could stop and exchange places when one of us got tired of pedaling even though both of us were on one bike. We made pretty good time. We finally arrived in Nashville, left the bicycle in a rack in front of Myers Theater (we didn't have need of a bicycle lock), and rushed up to the ticket booth. We fumbled for our dimes, at the same time asking if the show had started. "You're just in time. The main feature has just begun," the ticket lady assured us.

"Heck, we missed the previews," I said, shaking my head and looking at the posters advertising coming attractions.

"Come on or we'll miss the beginning," Dewey Lee admonished me, exasperated at my dawdling.

We stumbled in, stepping on toes, Dewey Lee almost sitting in someone's lap, until finally we found two vacant seats in the dark theater.

The show had already started. It was the story of a little girl named Dorothy, running into a house trying to get out of an awful storm. She got in the house OK, but it was blown by the wind up into the sky and fell down in a strange land where little people lived. Dorothy wanted to go home so badly that I really felt sorry for her. She finally met up with some strange-looking folks. One was a man full of straw called the Scarecrow, another was a Tin Man, and the other had a lion head and tail. They were a funny-looking bunch, but they were nice folks who wanted to help Dorothy get home.

Dewey Lee punched me and said, "Boy, ain't this a good show!" I readily agreed.

Well, it wasn't too long before we began to change our minds. The Wicked Witch of the West appeared. I was apprehensive, but Dewey Lee was terrified. "Let's go!" Dewey Lee nervously whispered.

"No, not now. We've already paid our good money to see this show, and that's all it is, Dewey Lee, a show." Dewey Lee didn't answer.

Finally the story became so interesting we found ourselves running up and down the yellow brick road with Dorothy and her strange friends, but every time the creepy, cackling witch appeared, Dewey Lee would move over in his seat a little closer to me, becoming so completely involved that once he even yelled, "Dern you, you witch!"

"Hush, Dewey Lee," I whispered, a little embarrassed and trying to act like I wasn't scared, pretending to be the hero type. As a matter of fact, I was almost as frightened as he was.

Believe me, we were both relieved when the wicked witch melted. The show finally came to an end, and we agreed that it was the best show we had ever seen.

Dewey Lee and I stretched and slowly walked out of the theater. To our horror the sun had long gone. It was dark. The movie had lasted much longer than we thought it would. We were absolutely terrified. There was only one way to the safety of our homes, and that was by way of the dreaded night ride up the Brinkley Hill.

Dewey Lee jerked the bike from the rack and jumped on. I scrambled to get on the crossbar, and off we went with Dewey Lee pedaling as fast as he could. The full moon began to peek through the thick woods, casting long shadows. A hazy fog floated up from the ground, and the only sound was the bike tires crunching over the dirt road. Neither of us said a word. Finally an exhausted Dewey Lee said, "I have to rest, I can't pedal no more."

We didn't even stop to change places; Dewey Lee just leaned to one side, and I crawled around, took his seat and the handlebars, and began to pedal urgently. We were to make this change several times before we reached home.

On one of these exchanges, Dewey Lee looked back over his shoulder and cried out, "I see the wicked witch on her broomstick flying across the moon, see! Look! See!"

Dewey Lee was panic-stricken. I stole a look over my shoulder trying to see what he was talking about. It was a bad time to look back. The bike tire swerved out of the wheel track and hit a sandbar. The bike, Dewey Lee, and I tumbled in the sand.

To tell you the truth, I thought I saw the witch, too. Maybe it was the power of suggestion, but who knows?

We wanted to be brave, and we were, for about ten seconds, time enough for us to get really, really scared. Dewey Lee was so unnerved that he pulled the bike out of the sand, jumped on it, and started without me. I yelled, "Are you crazy? Are you goin' by yourself?" That got his attention. Dewey Lee slapped on brakes, skidded into the same sandbar, and rolled in the sand for a second time. He sat up, spit the sand out of his mouth, and in a shaky voice said, "I'm sorry. I'm so scared I can't think straight."

Without a word, I jumped on the crossbar, and we were off again.

I soon learned that fear can cause you to act in strange ways. Dewey Lee and I started talking constantly to each other, about everything—that is, except our blood-curdling dash toward the Brinkley Hill and the possible confrontation with the Wicked Witch of the West.

We tried to fly by Elm Grove Church, but for some reason, just at the bottom of Brinkley Hill, we coasted slower and slower across the creek bridge until we came to a complete stop. Our eyes were wide with terror and fixed on the hill ahead.

I whispered, "Just like all them ghost stories we heard about. Everything's so quiet. No noise from the frogs, crickets, or nothin'." This kind of talk didn't help either one of us.

Dewey Lee, his voice trembling, said, "Let's go back."

"Go back where?" I questioned.

"I don't care where."

"If we go back and try to go home another way, it'll be day before we get there." I was trying to calm Dewey Lee. I think that helped me to stay calm. "It's just a hill. I don't believe all those stories," I lied.

"All right, but we'll have to run," Dewey Lee answered halfheartedly. "We can't pedal up the hill; it's too steep. And we'll have to take turns pushin' the bike."

We stood at the bottom of the hill for a minute or two, looking up. The moonlight was just enough for us to see ghostly rock shapes and creepy shadows of tall bushes leaning over ditches snaking down each side of the road.

"Enough!" I squeaked. My high-pitched voice startled both of us. I had a fleeting thought of the black thing on the back of Sam and Jeff's wagon at the very place we were standing. "Let's go!"

We started up the steep hill, me in one wheel track and Dewey Lee and the bike in the other. The Brinkley Hill was so steep that anyone would get tired just walking to the top, much less running all the way. We were so frightened and ran so fast that we were almost there when both of us stumbled to the ground, gasping for breath. After a brief rest we stood up. "My legs are shakin' so bad I can hardly stand up, but we've got to make it. We're not far from the top. If you're ready, I am," I said, almost out of breath.

Suddenly Dewey Lee screamed. I spun around. He was white as a field of cotton after the first frost, pointing a shaking finger at the bottom of the hill.

There stood the Wicked Witch of the West in her old floppy black hat and cloak, her chilling high-pitched laughter echoing up the creek. We both whirled around, ready to start running. This time we both screamed. Now the Wicked Witch was dancing around at the top, her piercing laughter echoing off the sides of the hill and down through the woods. Each of us was paralyzed. I found myself hyperventilating. Dewey Lee was hysterical. He kept saying over and over again. "Oh Lord, the witch is gonna get us! Oh Lord, the witch is gonna get us!"

I finally gathered enough strength to stagger over to him and yell right in his ear, "Dewey Lee, Dewey Lee, we got to run." He looked at me as if he were in a trance. I grabbed him in back of the head, pulled his face right up to mine and shouted, "We can get away from the witch. We can get away from the witch!"

Dewey Lee slowly blinked his eyes, shook his head and asked, "How?"

I didn't know how, so I said the first thing that came to my feeble, frightened mind, "We'll run up the hill, straight at her."

His answer was expected. "Are you crazy?"

"No, I don't think so. We can't climb up the steep sides of the hill. We could go back down and meet the witch at the creek. Not me. I'm running for home. That's up the hill. I'd rather meet the witch there. At least that's on the way home."

Dewey Lee looked one way and then the other. Between sobs he nodded his head in agreement, threw his bike in the ditch, and started running with me close behind, toward the witch and the top of the hill. When we got within a few feet of that horrible creature, to our astonishment and joy, she melted! We turned, looked back down the hill, and she was gone from there too, just like in the movie. We both dropped to our knees. I know I said a silent prayer of thanks, and I'm sure Dewey Lee did too.

Both of us sat down right there on top of the Brinkley Hill, perspiration mixed with tears trickling down our cheeks, thankfulness shining in our eyes. "Dewey Lee," I said, "You reckon we really saw what we thought we saw? You know what, it could have been a shadow and we just thought it was the witch."

"And a bird or something could have flown across the moon," Dewey Lee added hopefully.

"Well, anyway, if anybody finds out about this, we'll be the laughingstock of the whole neighborhood, and we'll be teased to death."

Dewey Lee quickly agreed, and we took a blood-brothers' oath never to tell, like Indians we had seen in a show, placing our wrists together, without the blood, of course. We got up to leave. "I ain't goin' back for my bike this night. I'll get up early in the morning and go get it," Dewey Lee said with a sheepish grin. I really didn't blame him.

Dewey Lee and I grew up together and often reminisced about our encounter with the Wicked Witch on the Brinkley Hill. We kept our oath, however. We never told, I guess, until now.

Dewey Lee has passed away now, but I am sure that, if he were here, he would say, "OK, you're released from the oath. Just don't say that I was more frightened than you." Heck, I just did, but you know what he would say to that? "I knew you would."

Well, there you have it. Another tale to add to the legends of the Brinkley Hill.

Tommy and Dewey Lee
Sworn Blood Brothers

CHAPTER NINETEEN

Spare the Rod

In today's world there is much discussion as to whether corporal punishment is appropriate for children. I'm sure my mother did not decide lightly, but, as you shall see, on occasion her decision came down on the side of the rod.

Daddy believed that my education was the most important thing in all of our lives. Well, my mother felt the same way, but her way of motivating me to learn was different from Daddy's. She would try other forms of discipline first. But if they didn't work, she was forced to turn to the old adage, "Spare the rod and spoil the child," as a last resort. It worked.

I learned how to study and got the education. I remember so well. Daddy was in his rocking chair by the little wood heater reading the newspaper, and Mother was busy in the kitchen. Daddy looked up at me from the newspaper and said, "Time for you to hit the books. I want you to be the best student in the third grade this year."

"Listen, Daddy, I already got up my lessons at school," I answered, my eyes shifting a bit at this obvious evasion.

Mother yelled out from the kitchen, "Go to the table and start your homework!"

We had a big, round table that sat in the den/dining room. It was used as a dinner table whenever the preacher came for Sunday dinner, but it served as my homework prison during the week. Even today when Beverly and I serve guests at this same table, my mind flits back to the nightly battles of my youth.

"OK, OK, I'm going, Mother," I sighed and sat, reluctantly opening my books. Boy, was I the great pretender when it came to actually studying. I'd fiddle with the pages, my eyes glazing over, remembering the hoofbeats of the great horse Silver. The Lone Ranger rides again! No one could tell exactly what I was doing, that is, except Mother. When she saw that I was daydreaming she would drop the dishcloth, sit down with me, and read the lesson aloud. Then she would ask me questions about what she had read. But I was stubborn. Sometimes I couldn't or wouldn't answer.

"All right, young man. I can't make you study, but I can certainly make you sit there!" Sometimes that approach would work, and sometimes it wouldn't.

Many times Mother would sit by me and cry when I refused to do my homework. Seeing the tears rolling down her cheeks, I, too, would begin to cry. The tears would end with a hug, and by that time I would usually be motivated to begin my studies in earnest. But there were times when even her tears did not work.

One day I was in a particularly bad mood (Mother called it headstrong). With all Mother's urging, pleading, and crying, I simply refused to do schoolwork. Mother left the room. I grinned, thinking that she had given up, but I should have known better. I continued sitting at the table daydreaming and absentmindedly rolling a little toy truck back and forth over my books when suddenly a searing, stinging pain flashed across my back. I screamed, looking around to find my tearful mother standing behind me, holding a thin, limber switch.

Well, I guess Mother had accepted the wisdom of the instruction "Spare the rod and spoil the child." Thank goodness she used a slender switch, not a rod. I got the message, and after that switching and crying scene, she never had to switch me again.

As a matter of fact, Mother switched me only two times in my life: that third-grade homework switching and the "Willie Ed" switching when I was four years old. I can't see why she did that. It was only the fourth time I had disobeyed her and run away to play with Willie Ed's children!

I must admit that I probably needed more than two whippings in my younger days, but my mother was kind as well as strict. I know now, more than ever, that she was the best mother in the world. No telling how I would have turned out if I had not had such loving, motivated parents. It is fitting that I refer to them many times in my writings for, after all, I've become who I am because of them.

The Preacher Comes to Dinner

IF THE OLD DINING ROOM table could talk or even write a book, it could reveal more of the Cooper family life than I can. For it was around this table that life's problems, large and small, were debated, where laughter was interspersed with serious discussion, where quiet times were interrupted only by the snap of a mousetrap in the pantry and the giggle of the little boy who set the trap. That old table could tell of the merriment of Christmas, the smell of cedar, the squeal of delight and happiness over the secondhand but well-repaired bicycle found under the tree, and the list goes on.

Well, old table, I'm going to tell one on you, and I do mean "on" you.

Mother was always involved in church work, and from time to time young ministerial students from Wake Forest College would come down to preach at Elm Grove Baptist Church. The ladies of the church would take turns inviting the preacher to dinner. And remember, that's what we call "lunch" today.

On this Sunday it was Mother's turn to have the preacher for dinner. She was up before daybreak, cooking and getting ready for the big event. In those days, taking a guest out to a restaurant was unheard of. In fact, restaurants were unheard of. A woman expressed her inner soul in the kitchen, and her talent or artistic skill at preparing a meal was her way of guaranteeing appreciation from her man and from the community at large. At mealtime, she was queen.

You can be sure that my mother was always in the race for approval, and you can be doubly sure that she was a safe bet to win. Today's woman doesn't have to depend on the frying pan to make her place in the family indispensable. Whether Mother knew it or not, she didn't really have to depend on it either. But cooking was her specialty.

Daddy seldom went to church, but whenever we had the preacher for dinner, he was expected to go. Daddy was certainly the boss of the family, but on this issue he somehow knew it was useless to protest.

After church on this particular Sunday, Daddy, the preacher, and I were sitting around the old dining room table making small talk while Mother trotted in and out of the kitchen bringing dish after dish of vegetables, ham, chicken, beef stew, biscuits. I know I have missed a few other dishes, but you get the picture.

Mother finally sat down to join us for dinner and asked the preacher to say the blessing. When the "Amen" finally came, all of us were nearly starving. But just as Daddy reached for the steaming bowl of butterbeans to pass to the preacher, Mother jumped up, saying, "I forgot the iced tea!" She stood up so quickly that she knocked one of the cross braces under the table loose.

Then, to our horror, burdened by the weight of so many dishes piled high with nourishment from the kitchen, the old table just gave up. The tabletop buckled, tilting downward like the *Titanic*, sliding dishes into the laps of Daddy and the preacher. There was a mad scramble with everyone grabbing plates of corn on the cob and fried chicken legs, trying to keep the skidding bowls from hitting the floor.

After only one or two dishes had escaped us, Daddy yelled to the preacher and me, "Quick! Spread out your arms as wide as you can on the table in front of the food!" We followed instructions and, sure enough, that tactic corralled the stampeding dishes and kept them from tumbling to the floor. Daddy slowly moved his knees up under the table until it was level. I was then instructed to move a little side table up under the broken crossbeam. This did the trick.

The dining room table was level again, and we simply slid our chairs and empty plates around, ready for the feast. No one said anything while Mother gathered baked sweet potatoes off the floor and returned them to the kitchen. Faces were expressionless. Then, after an awkward moment of silence, Mother shyly inquired, "May I pass the butterbeans to anyone?"

Believe it or not, everybody burst out laughing. I think the preacher laughed loudest.

The very next Sunday the same young preacher came to conduct the morning service. After the opening hymn, he walked to the pulpit with a grin on his face and said, "As you know, it is the usual practice of the ladies of this church to invite visiting preachers for Sunday dinner. Well, last Sunday, it was my privilege to have been invited to the home of the Miss Lois Cooper family. The meal was simply delicious. I'm a big eater, and I'm sometimes afraid that I'll eat over my share of the food. Well, at Miss Lois's dinner, I did not have this worry. In fact, there was so much food on the table that the table broke down!" This announcement was greeted by disbelieving laughter, and he continued, "It's the truth! And only the quick thinking of Mr. Roy saved a meal that I enjoyed immensely. Thank you, Miss Lois, for a truly memorable Sunday dinner."

At this point, the entire congregation turned to look admiringly at Mother, who blushed with pleasure at this public recognition of her kitchen prowess.

Remember, I told you at the beginning of this little tale that, if the old dining room table could talk or write a book, it could tell you more about Cooper family life than I ever could.

You know, I wonder if the old table was jealous and fell down on purpose, knowing that I should at least give it some place of prominence in the Cooper family life. I believe that the old table is now satisfied and won't fall down again within the foreseeable future. We can relax and enjoy our Thanksgiving dinners!

Spilt Milk

IN MY EARLY boyhood days, there was little in our pantry that had been bought from a grocery store. Mother found the pennies for a few luxury items like coffee, tea, salt, sugar, and sometimes King's syrup. And of course Daddy, an iced tea lover, always had to make a trip to the ice house in Nashville. Five cents bought him a five-pound block of ice which he wrapped in fertilizer bags and stored under the house, the coolest spot he could find in the hot days of summer.

Later we bought an insulated ice box, which doubled as an end table. That was a real step up the ladder, I thought. I can't remember exactly, but I was at least eight years old before Carolina Power and Light Company found the way to our house with electricity.

Mother and Daddy were a hard-working pair, devoted to their only child and determined to make a better life for me. Daddy, the supervisor of the farming operation, led the pack and never asked anyone to do anything he wouldn't do.

On the other hand, my mother was the captain of the household chores. Not only captain, but chief cook and bottle washer and deckhand and any other position you care to name. For example, she washed and ironed all our clothes the hard way. She didn't throw them in the washing machine and dryer or take them to the cleaners.

Instead, she built a fire around a heavy black wash pot filled with water to boil our clothes. After rubbing the hot, soaped clothes on an aluminum washboard and rinsing them in the boiling water, she carefully pinned each item on the clothesline to dry. Ironing came next, but there was no electricity to heat the flatirons. She put them on the stove to get them hot enough to iron out the wrinkles and put a crease in our pants.

But washing and ironing were just part of Mother's tasks. Her primary responsibility was keeping food on our table, a job that required endless planning and daily setbacks. For example, preserving summer vegetables and fruits grown on our farm by canning was huge. Remember, we had no freezer!

But there were canning hazards that even Mother couldn't avoid. One morning is still fresh in my memory. As usual, before I could open my eyes, Mother's voice floated into my semiconscious mind. "Time to get up, honey. You've got to milk the cow, and you don't want to miss the school bus."

I groaned and rolled over. When I got my eyes adjusted, I saw by the old clock on the mantle that it was just a quarter to six. "Mother," I yelled, "you're not supposed to call me until six o'clock."

"I'm sorry, son. The clock in the kitchen must be fast. Anyway, I've already fixed your breakfast so you won't have to gobble it down."

After a long stretch and with great effort, I threw back the covers, pulled on my clothes, and started for the kitchen. "Morning, Mother," I yawned. "I'm hungry. Please pass those good-smelling biscuits."

"Well, good morning, sleepyhead," she greeted me. "These are your favorites, sweet potato biscuits. How many do you want?"

"I'll take three, and please pass the butter!" That butter, of course, was homemade.

At that moment there was a loud pop on the back porch. "Oh no!" Mother groaned. "Not again." We hurried to the screened-in back porch where Mother kept house-length rows of half-gallon jars filled with corn, butterbeans, tomatoes, peas, peppers, pickles, preserves, jellies, and berries of all types. Today's grocery store canned goods shelf has nothing on Mother's back porch display.

But this morning Mother looked with dismay at a half-gallon jar once filled to the brim with freshly cooked corn, now half empty. Corn was splattered on the floor, on the walls, on the ceiling, and was plastered to the back porch screen.

"Tommy, go back in the kitchen and finish your breakfast before you go milk the cow. It'll take me at least an hour to clean up this mess."

As I wrote this little narrative I realized I was puzzled as to why some of Mother's jar lids exploded while most of the others did not. So I did some research. I remembered that, as a child, I had discussed this matter with several of the mothers in the neighborhood. Some said it was because whatever they were cooking was not cooked enough or that the lid was sealed too tightly or not tightly enough or there wasn't enough space left at the top of the jar for the contents to expand.

All of these explanations seemed valid, but I wanted to know for sure which one was correct, so before I finished this story I headed for the computer. The answer I found matched one of the neighborhood mother's explanations. Items such as corn and butterbeans tend to swell and explode if they don't have enough room. After eighty years, I finally found the answer to my question.

After inspecting the clean-up needed on the back porch, Mother and I returned to the kitchen. By that time, the biscuits were cold. I had looked forward to those hot potato biscuits. Sopping molasses with cold potato biscuits and eating cold fatback was not what I had envisioned just before the untimely explosion.

While I was finishing my breakfast, Mother was scrubbing my already clean aluminum milk bucket. She filled another sparkling bucket half full of warm water and dropped in two white rags, sterile I'm sure, to be used to wash the tits and bag of Daisy, our cow. Mother was noted for her absolute cleanliness rule. I didn't realize then just how smart she was.

"And you got up fifteen minutes early. It's a shame. You had a cold breakfast and now you've got to rush to milk the cow and get ready to catch the school bus," Mother sighed with disgust.

"Don't worry, Mother. I've got plenty of time," I assured her. I'd had the milking job for a year, and at the age of nine I thought I had things under control. How little I knew!

I finished breakfast, snatched the two buckets and rags, and hurried down the path toward the cow pasture, grumbling all the way. "Got up early, corn volcano, cold breakfast, what else!" I was soon to find out.

As I neared the pasture, Old Daisy poked her head over the barbed-wire fence, her big eyes following me every step of the way to the corncrib where I filled a bucket with cottonseed meal and hulls.

Old Daisy was free to roam in a big barbed wire pasture with six mules. The barbed wire enclosed all of a big two-story building except for the front where the doors were located. Although we called this building the corncrib, it should have been called the feed barn. It contained not only corn, but sacks of Red Dog for the hogs; oats, fodder, and cottonseed hulls for the cows; and bales of hay piled high in the loft for the mules.

Daisy's feed trough was nailed to the outside of the crib in the pasture. Each morning I had to leave my two buckets outside of the pasture, go in the crib to get a bucket of feed, carry it through the barbed-wire fence, and empty it in the trough. I always had to avoid Daisy's pushing and nuzzling attempts to eat out of the bucket as I carried it to the trough.

Well, this particular morning, Old Daisy saw me coming down the path and jogged over to the feed trough as usual. She looked at me with those big round eyes, constantly licking her lips all around her mouth, walking back and forth from her feed box to the barbed-wire fence where she knew I would be coming with her favorite breakfast.

Getting through the barbed-wire fence with a bucket of feed was usually enough of a challenge for me. But on this morning, my rush to finish the job and Daisy's enthusiasm for breakfast spelled disaster.

As I swung my leg recklessly through the fence, the prickly barbs snagged my pants leg and trapped me. At that very moment, Daisy, impatient for her chow, lowered her head and aimed right for the bucket of cottonseed meal and hulls that I clutched in my hands.

But before I could even let loose a useless "*No!*" Daisy, who had her own plans, butted the bucket with a vigorous swoop of her head, sending about half of the meal and hulls flying everywhere.

Well, I won't tell you what I said as I freed myself from the barbs, but it certainly wasn't appropriate for a little nine-year-old boy. Angrily, I poured the few remaining contents of the bucket into the trough. Then I tried to brush the meal out of my hair and rub Daisy's disgusting, yellow cowlick off my torn pants leg.

At that point, completely fed up, I decided to get on with the morning's chore. With one last glance at all that good feed, now useless, scattered all over the ground, I grabbed my two buckets from the other side of the fence and pulled up a small three-legged stool from under the trough. At last, I was ready to do some milking.

I washed Daisy's udders and big, puffy bag with the now not-so-warm water and one of the two clean rags Mother had provided. Old Daisy just glanced at me with that look in her eyes which assured me, "The water's all right, *this* time." I quickly dried her with the other rag. With my little stool in just the right position and the milk bucket placed carefully under Daisy's udders, I placed my hands on two tits and began pulling first with one hand and then the other. The milk began making a little sing-song noise as it streamed from each faucet and hit the bottom of the milk bucket.

Just as I got my rhythm, Old Daisy turned her head and looked at me. I knew what she was saying. "Tommy, there's a horse fly circling my tail, and I think it's about to land on me. Please shoo it away."

I craned my neck around to inspect her rear end and stood up to look over her back. Nothing. Not even a mosquito. Thinking that I had misinterpreted her look, I sat down and continued milking.

However, when my bucket was about half full, Old Daisy, using her tail as a whip, lashed my back, simultaneously lifting her right leg and kicking it out with the swiftness and fury of a lightning bolt. The horse fly buzzed off in terror. I jumped back and watched, helpless and horror-struck, as she gingerly placed her kicking foot smack dab in the bottom of the milk bucket.

I went stark-raving mad, not insane, for I knew what I was doing when I hit Old Daisy in the side with my fist. I think I just lost my sense of reason. Old Daisy bellowed, ran a short distance from the milking site, looked back at me, her soulful eyes filled with disbelief. I could almost hear her crying, "I can't believe you did that."

"Well, Daisy," I mumbled, "I can't believe it either, but you didn't have to put your foot in the milk bucket!"

Finally, an apprehensive Old Daisy, forgiving, hungry soul that she was, walked slowly back to the feed trough and soon began gobbling her feed as if nothing had happened.

As I looked down at my half-full milk bucket, I was dumbfounded. Why had Daisy done such a thing? She had kicked the bucket over before but she had never put her foot right in the milk! Was it an accident or was it a clever act of retaliation? After all, I hadn't spotted the horsefly on her rump. I would never know, but the primary question at that moment was what I could do about my predicament.

I had several choices. I could carry an empty bucket back to the house and incur the wrath of my mother, who was depending on a full bucket of fresh milk to churn our butter for the coming week. I could keep standing there, or I could go back to the house for a clean bucket, miss the school bus, and probably put my father in a rage. What to do? "Hey, I've got an idea. I know exactly what to do," I assured myself.

Quickly I began sloshing the milk around to clean the bucket, turned it upside down to drain every drop of dirty milk, inspected for any telltale signs of Daisy's foot, and dropped down on the stool to milk the other half bucket I knew Daisy could provide. *This is easy,* I thought. *Mother'll believe I tripped and spilled half a bucket. At least she can churn half the butter we need, and maybe she won't be so mad with me.*

Leaving the milking stool and rag bucket propped against the barn, I grabbed the bucket half full of milk and rushed up the path. But as I neared the house, the questions that had been dormant in my mind slowly began to arise. *Should I tell Mother that Daisy stepped in the milk bucket? Was the milk safe to drink? What would Mother do if I told her?* With these agonizing thoughts, my hurried gait toward the house got slower and slower. *If I don't tell her anything, that's certainly not telling her a lie. So what's wrong with that?* Nothing. Problem solved.

When I reached the house Mother was standing on the back porch holding the screen door open for me. The sun was just peeking over the trees, the morning dew still on the grass. It was a little cold to me, but not to Mother. The whites of her blue eyes were streaked with red. Perspiration was running down her face, pooling around her neck, and soaking her dress. "I just finished cleaning up this mess. Corn was stuck all over everything!" Mother complained, glancing up quickly for sympathy. Her eyes widened. The sight of me was too much. "What happened to you? Your pants are torn, and your shirt's filthy," she exclaimed as she grabbed the handle of the milk bucket.

The light weight of the pail startled her, and she quickly shifted her attention to the result of my morning's labor, only half a bucket of milk. "Don't tell me the cow kicked the bucket over again!"

"Yes'um," I mumbled. *Hmmm, this is going to be easier than I thought.*

"And I suppose it got a little dirt in it like last time."

As usual Mother was right on the money. I didn't answer.

"I know accidents can happen, but this is the third time. You're just careless!"

I could tell she was mad.

"Answer me. Did you get any dirt in the bucket?"

"Not exactly." *That was safe. It was Daisy, not me, who got the dirt in the bucket!*

"There's no 'not exactly.' Did any dirt get in the bucket or not?" *Uh-oh. Bad question.* I could tell Mother was really getting mad.

"Not when she kicked the bucket. I held on to it," I ventured. I knew by the time I said it, that answer was stupid!

"Well, just how did dirt get in the milk?"

"Mother, the milk's clean. I used half of it to clean the bucket."

Mother's voice softened into what seemed to me the low snarl of an attacking tiger. "Well, just why did you have to wash the bucket with half the milk?"

"Mother, I thought about it all the way to the house. I didn't want to tell you, but I know better than to tell you a lie. Old Daisy stepped in the bucket when it was about half full of milk. I had to clean it out before I could finish milking."

"So now you think you have a clean bucket of milk. I don't think so." Turning from me in disgust, Mother flung the contents of the bucket into the backyard and whirled around, her finger pointed straight at my nose. "Get in the house. Take off those torn pants and that filthy shirt. Look in the closet and get a clean shirt and pair of pants. Don't forget your book sack. Come back down here so I can comb your hair. You don't have but five minutes to catch the bus. Move! Now!"

I quickly ran to the closet in the bedroom, dressed, grabbed my book sack, and returned to the kitchen where Mother was waiting with comb and brush in hand.

"We have to hurry. You'll have to run to Pat's." The Nashville School bus always picked me up on the road at the bottom of the hill ditches in front of Aunt Pat's. Mother pulled me close and quickly began to comb my hair. Yes, she still did that, but this time the comb caught in the tangles and spun to the floor.

Mother, at the end of her patience, pulled back her hand and slapped me on the cheek. She had spanked me before, but never before had she slapped me in the face. We were both surprised, but after the first shock, she put her arms around me and hugged me tightly. I wasn't physically hurt, only my feelings. I felt the way Old Daisy must have felt when I smacked her. Both of us babbled through tears, "I'm so sorry. I didn't mean to do it." She never slapped my face again although I probably deserved it. She gave me a quick love lick on the fanny, and I jumped off the porch.

It didn't take but a few minutes for me to run to the end of the path where Alvin Joyner and Janice and Peggy Cooper had just boarded the school bus. The driver, J. B. Rose, reopened the door, grinned, and said, "Just a little late, aren't you?"

"You don't know the half of it, J.B.," I sighed, sinking gratefully into my seat.

As I remember, the school day went well, and Old Daisy and I got along just fine as I continued to do my share of the chores that kept the Cooper farm afloat. But I must admit I'll never forget that terrible morning.

As the years passed, college and law school relieved me of the farm chores I grew up with. Daddy's heart attack reduced him to watching TV or sitting around Cuther Watson's store in our old country neighborhood. Mother died at the age of ninety-two, but she never slowed down. Those hands stayed busy until the very end. We all could use a bit of her stamina.

Mother is always the first one out for church

CHAPTER TWENTY

Fishin'

IN THE 1930s Nash County creeks and streams were teaming with life: fish, minnows, turtles, snakes, you name it. I didn't drink creek water without boiling it, but I probably could have. As a matter of fact, when we worked in the backfields located along a ridge above the creek, we drank water from a spring located just two hundred yards from the creek, the crystal-clear water bubbling out of the ground at the base of a sweet gum tree.

We would always rush for the gourd dippers hanging nearby to quench our thirst and take a minute or so to rest after working under the blazing sun. Each time, however, we had to wait impatiently for the clean white sand on the bottom of the spring to settle. The bullfrog that lived nearby almost always jumped in the water when he saw us coming!

I certainly waded, swam, and, most fun of all, fished in the sparkling-clear streams and creeks that dotted the Elm Grove countryside. Any chance I got I headed out with every intention of snagging a few fish for my mother to batter and fry.

On the few days when we had caught up on our work, mostly on Saturdays, I would head to the creek with my reed fishing pole, hook, and sinker. I had an extra hook firmly stuck in the end of a corncob to prevent it from hooking me when I placed it in my back pocket along with a paper sack filled with tiny white slices of white hog meat my mother had cut up as bait. No fish could resist this tasty morsel. With gear intact, I would be off to fish for redfins, a member of the jackfish family, distinguished by bright red, as opposed to black, fins. Everybody called this exciting pastime "redfinning."

For me there was nothing better than trolling alone along the banks of Little Sapony in the back woods. Here the clear waters of the creek ran snakelike for at least three miles before slithering under the bridge on the Old Bailey Road at the bottom of the Brinkley Hill.

The tall trees shielded the forest floor except at a few spots. Trees were much smaller along the creek where the sun seeped in. Some of these smaller trees leaned over the creek as if they were looking at themselves in a mirror.

On this particular Saturday morning there was complete silence, broken only by the machine-gun-fire bursts of a yellow hammer woodpecker on a hollow tree somewhere high up on a ridge above the creek. As soon as I reached my favorite spot I unwound my line from my fishing pole and carefully baited the hook with the white meat Mother had prepared for me, arranging it so that a narrow slice would hang down.

When fishing for most other fish I used a cork that floated on the surface of the water that either dipped down when a fish nibbled or completely disappeared when a fish took the bait. When the cork sank, I knew to jerk my pole and pull my catch out of the water.

In fishing for redfin, however, I didn't use a cork. The best redfin fishing was in rapidly moving water where a cork was useless. As the water swirled around my line, I moved my pole up and down, causing the narrow hanging slice of white meat to wigwag, imitating a wiggling worm or a fluttering insect. As you can see, redfinning was the precursor of fly fishing; at least that's the way it seems to me.

With my fishing pole and baited hook I stood for a moment in the sunshine, which filtered through the trees in the quietness of the woods, disturbed only by the murmur of the waters farther down the creek. I was spellbound, but only for a moment. The splashing of the water meant that up ahead, the water was running faster, and in the deep pool, past the rocks, the redfins would be feeding.

I panicked. I never was a calm fisherman which, I'm sure, is no surprise to anyone who knows me. In the rush to get down the creek where I knew the redfins were waiting with open mouths, I ran as fast as my legs would carry me. Suddenly something grabbed my fishing pole and jerked it out of my hands. I was stunned. Jerking my head around, I found my fishing pole hanging defiantly from a limb, secured tightly by my fishing line.

I jerked the line so hard that the fishing hook embedded itself in the tree limb, and, of course, I broke the line. With the loss of my hook and left with a tangled, broken fishing line, I was, to put it mildly, furious. I said unkind words to the limb, hook, and line: "You dern rascal! Fool! You hateful thing!" Strange that back then neither my close country childhood friends nor I ever used the profanity that seems to be prevalent with children and adults today.

Well, having vented my wrath, I slowly picked up my pole and carefully began to untangle the fishing line in order to tie it to my extra hook and to the pole. With that task completed I began to trot down the creek toward the swift waters, being extra careful to keep glancing back to be certain no hanging limbs would grab my pole off my shoulder again.

But trouble can come from any direction. All of a sudden my feet got tangled up in what I thought was a limb until I looked down. A water moccasin was thrusting its tail against my legs. It's a shame that I wasn't competing in a school jumping contest. I would have won hands down. I let out a scream and headed upward. I don't know who was more afraid, me or the snake. When I came down, the water moccasin, one of the deadliest snakes in the area, had long ago plunged into the creek, headed for home. I paused, heart pounding. With the snake episode still very much on my mind, one of my five senses—my hearing—had been turned off but suddenly awoke to the sweet roaring sound of a waterfall.

The falling water had been formed when a dead tree had fallen into the creek. Its branches had collected all sorts of debris like tree limbs, trash, rocks big and small, and, on top of that, sand. With the passing of time, growing roots from nearby trees had built a dam, which created a pond of rapidly flowing water, home for redfins large and small, all hungrily waiting for the white tender morsels my mother had lovingly prepared.

With the thrill and excitement only a country boy in the 1930s could possibly experience, I dropped to the ground, opened my paper sack, and with trembling hands affixed the magical bait. There was no question in my mind that Mother's expectations would be fulfilled and that we would have a fish supper fit for a king. I was right!

CHAPTER TWENTY-ONE

Fish Whisperer

WILLIE ED, his wife Margaret, their three children, and Willie Ed's mother—or Aunt Jennie, as everyone called her—all lived in a little four-room house on the path that led by my four-room house and down the hill ditches to Little Sapony Creek.

Aunt Jennie was tall like Willie Ed, a big woman. Not fat, not muscular, just big. I remember her beautiful white teeth and the deepening of the grooves in her only two wrinkles when she smiled, which was often. Her snow white hair, contrasting sharply with her charcoal skin, was short and wavy, a style achieved by home scissors, I'm sure. I know she didn't go to the beauty parlor.

Aunt Jennie never seemed to tire of the many children hanging around her house. You remember that's why I got my second whipping, running away for the fourth time to play with Willie Ed's children. She gave us sweets she knew we liked and never had a harsh word for any of us even when we must have tried her patience. I remember once she even sewed up a hole I had torn in my breeches playing under her house.

In early spring and into the late days of August, it was not unusual to see Aunt Jennie walking down the road toward Little Sapony Creek, carrying in one hand a fishing pole and a hoe and in the other hand a bucket and a small, wooden three-legged stool. Aunt Jennie loved fishing, and her favorite spot was near the bridge that crosses the creek at the bottom of the Brinkley Hill.

Her ability to catch fish almost every time she put her hook in the water was a community legend. She seemed to know where the fish were and what bait they wanted. Only a "fish whisperer," able to communicate with these finny creatures, could accomplish that feat.

One Saturday afternoon, Dewey Lee, Allen, and I were at the creek with fishing poles, lines, and hooks baited with freshly dug, fat, and juicy fishing worms. We flung our lines out as far as we could and sat down on the bank, each intently watching his cork. If it bobbled the least bit, we were on our feet filled with wide-eyed excitement, ready to pull up a big yellow-belly perch should the cork sink below the surface of the water. That day it didn't happen.

We fished and fished, but none of us had a single nibble. "They're just not biting," Allen said with disgust.

"Well," Dewey Lee added, "we should have come earlier in the morning. Ain't nobody can catch fish this time of day. It's just too hot."

"Maybe Aunt Jennie done caught 'em all," I added morosely.

"You young'uns ought to know ain't nobody, includin' me, can catch all the fish in this creek," Aunt Jennie muttered as she walked up quietly behind us.

We all jumped. "Good grief, Aunt Jennie, you scared us!" I muttered.

"You just hafta be patient," she continued. "Dat's the trouble nowadays, folks just ain't got no patience for nothing." All the while she was unwinding her fishing pole and baiting her hook with a big wiggling fishing worm. Then, to our astonishment, she spit on her hook!

We looked at each other. Had we discovered Aunt Jennie's secret? We stared as she tossed her line near the center of the creek and settled down on her three-legged stool to await what we hoped was a sure thing.

Trying not to be noticed, almost in unison, we pulled our hooks out of the water, spit on the baited hooks, and confidently threw our lines back, believing that our newly spit-upon bait would be irresistible and that the fish would be waiting with open mouths. This expectation was confirmed when Aunt Jennie's cork dived beneath the surface of the water. She stood up quickly and expertly landed a big yellow-belly perch on the creek bank.

Now we knew for sure that we had discovered Aunt Jennie's secret. To make doubly certain that our hooks were properly lubricated, however, we withdrew them again and saturated them with our spit.

With our freshly soaked bait in the water we began to fish in earnest, watching intently for the slightest ripple, the tiniest sign of movement. We fished for at least thirty minutes but without a single nibble. Our corks seemed to have been planted in concrete.

Hearing Aunt Jennie shift her weight on her three-legged stool, preparing to stand, we turned to look for her cork. It was nowhere in sight. She slowly arose and pulled another perch from the creek, this one a little bigger than the first.

When Aunt Jennie repeated her performance for a third time, it was difficult to hide our disappointment. None of us said anything. The silence was broken only by Aunt Jennie's soft chuckle. After a few more minutes of floating corks and still waters, Allen whispered, "I know why she's catching all those fish, and we're not getting a single bite."

Dewey Lee and I blurted hoarsely, "Why?"

"Look over there where she's sittin'. See that old rotten tree stump settin' in the creek about four feet from the bank? I bet there's a whole school of fish around that stump!"

“It sure looks like a perfect place to fish,” I ventured. Dewey nodded a “yes” and moved a little closer to the tree stump and to Aunt Jennie.

Allen pulled in his hook and line and strolled casually around Dewey Lee, Aunt Jennie, and the old stump. Taking my hook and line out of the water, I walked past Dewey Lee and sidled closer to Aunt Jennie before throwing my hook out into the creek as near as I could to the old rotten stump. Our new positions near Aunt Jennie and the stump made us a sure bet, or so we thought. Any passerby could have read our positive thoughts from the happy, expectant expressions on our faces.

Time passed slowly though. We began to think the hourglass had clogged, when lo and behold Aunt Jennie stood up. You guessed it. Another fat yellow-belly perch was flapping at the end of her line. No one spoke. She spit and threw in her hook and line again. We all three inched closer to Aunt Jennie until the three of us were almost sitting with her on her little three-legged stool.

She looked at us with sorrow and a tinge of disgust. “All right, young’uns, you can have this spot if that’s what you want. But, believe me, there’s fish all up and down this creek.” Aunt Jennie with stool, bucket filled with splashing perch, pole, line, and hook in tow moved about fifteen yards farther down the creek bank and settled down to fish.

The three of us immediately formed a tight triangle just across from the stump, haven to scores of yellow-belly perch, confident that we would pull in at least twice as many fish as Aunt Jennie had caught. Not a nibble. Not even one nibble among us.

Wafting on a quiet breeze from down creek came the sound of a soft chuckle and a fat fish belly flapping on the creek bank. “Mighty fine one there. One mo’, and I’ll have enough for supper. Told y’all there's plenty of fish in this creek! Just takes patience, that's all. Patience."

We looked at each other in resignation, slowly wound up our fishing gear, threw our poles over our shoulders, and started up the road home. Yes, there were many fish in the creek, but when Aunt Jennie was around, they bit nobody's hook but hers.

We never learned Aunt Jennie's secret, but in recent years as I began to understand the concept of horse whisperer and ghost whisperer, I finally figured it out. Although I never had that special communication with fish, hope springs eternal. To this day whenever I fish I always spit on the bait. It just seems the right thing to do.

CHAPTER TWENTY-TWO

Big Log

JACKFISH TENDED TO grow much larger than redfins and, of course, had no red fins. While redfins jumped on white pork meat, the bait jackfish couldn't resist was tasty little live roaches. Not the cockroaches that creep around your kitchen at night, but small fish we called roaches and some call minnows. In my time and in my neck of the woods, we more precisely called them "shad roaches."

Most all branches, the little streams that fed the creeks, were filled with schools of shad roaches. These tiny streams were a safe haven that protected the roaches from becoming lunch for the big fish, but didn't protect them from Allen and me.

I remember well one July day that was too hot for Allen and me to ride our bikes for very long. After climbing the hill ditches on the path to my house, we arrived in the front yard, dropped our bikes, and plopped down on one of the big oak roots under the welcome shade of the twin oak trees.

As you might have guessed, two ten-year-old boys don't just sit around and do nothing for very long.

"I know it's better to seine for roaches in the morning when it's cool like we had planned, but heck, let's try it now. Anyway, by the time we get our seine ready it ought to be cooler. We can go right behind your house and catch all the roaches we need, and we'll have more time tomorrow to go to the Big Log." Allen wiped the cooling sweat from his brow with the one dry spot he had located on his shirt.

"That suits me. We can use the same bag that we used the last time. You know, the Golden Bell Fertilizer bag that we split open to make it wide just like a real seine."

"Good," Allen replied. "Now all we need is a bucket. We can fill it with water from the branch to keep the roaches alive, and in the morning we'll be ready to go to the Big Log to catch a mess of jackfish."

The Big Log, located about two-and-a-half miles from the Creek Bridge at the bottom of the Brinkley Hill, was actually a pond filled with fresh dark water, formed by the widening of the creek. The area was almost completely sheltered from the sun by large cypress trees. Cypress knees were growing on the banks and underwater in the creek. We nicknamed the underwater ones "hook losers" in honor of all the unsuspecting fishing hooks that got caught in them and were lost forever.

When I was a young country boy, the spring branches, creeks, sloughs, and the woodlands through which they ran were my laboratory, and I was filled with curiosity about everything. For example, I wondered whether the cypress knees were a part of the cypress tree root, and, if so, what was their purpose? When I began writing this section, I realized that I had never answered that question. Thanks once again to the computer, I read that "the bizarrely twisted knees . . . grow out of the roots of cypress trees." But I still don't know their purpose.

Numerous small cypress logs fell from time to time across the pond and contributed to the slow flow of the water to the creek outlet, but the huge log that had fallen right in the middle of the pond long ago inspired the name "Big Log." As you might surmise, that log provided a cool recreation spot for two little country boys and some pretty big jackfish!

The next morning Allen came by my house, and together we carefully planned our trip to the Big Log. It would be a long walk that would take us to the bottom of the Brinkley Hill and from there along the run of the creek in an easterly direction. We packed the sandwiches our mothers had made for us, and after we filled two quart jars with water Allen had drawn from the well, we were well provisioned for the trek.

Next we hoisted on our shoulders two poles, lines, and enough hooks to feed the underwater cypress knots that would always catch several hooks and break our lines. Then there was the bait, the roaches we had seined the afternoon before, darting back and forth in a large bucket filled with cool water to keep them fresh. "How the heck are we going to carry all this?" I stammered.

Allen and I thought a few seconds, then blurted out, almost simultaneously, "Take turns!"

"Yeah," Allen grinned. "We'll have to remember that. It's always a good solution! We'll just trade the bucket back and forth. You carry it five minutes, and I'll carry it five minutes."

"I'll take it first," I offered. "Let's go."

We started out at a fast pace, exchanging the bucket about every five minutes. I say "about." Neither one of us had a watch, nor did any of the other kids at that time. Only grown men had watches that they carried in a small overall pocket attached by a U-shaped chain to another little pocket, assuring them that a dropped watch would be caught by one pocket or the other.

Actually we carried the buckets until one of us got tired. Then we would pass it to the other. The occasional patches of briars that we encountered along the creek hindered our progress. Allen and I had not been to the Big Log since the previous summer, and we had forgotten that in a few places the briars were so thick that they would grab our pants legs. Some of the taller briars would leap on our backs as if they were magnets and we were metal. These briars would cut, scratch, and tear our clothes, along with stinging cuts to our skin.

Carrying a bucket filled with water and live roaches was not a walk in the park, as they say. "Hey," Allen yelled, obviously in pain. "I'm caught. Take the bucket! Take the bucket!"

"I will! I will!' I assured him. "Just as soon as I can get free of these darned things myself!"

So it went. We had to replenish some of the bucket water from the creek a number of times, finally arriving at the Big Log with our fishing poles and hooks and, thank the Lord, our bucket full of water and live bait. Even though, on arrival, we were wringing wet with sweat, so tired that our knees were shaking, the mere sight of the Big Log under the umbrella of the big cypress trees made us forget our wet clothes and trembling knees. Our fatigue completely melted away when we heard a familiar splashing sound and saw a big jackfish jump clear of the water.

You can bet that we immediately dropped to our knees and began untangling our fishing lines and baiting our hooks. To accomplish that task, we reached down in the bucket of water among the roaches darting back and forth in a futile effort to escape our hands. When we captured one, its agony was not over. In fact, it had just begun. We plunged a hook into the back of each roach selected for bait, not far enough to kill it but just far enough so that it could continue to wiggle and swim around when we threw the hook and line into the water. The jackfish, never suspecting the trap, could not restrain his natural impulse to grab the helpless little roach for a delicious meal.

I know this baiting procedure will disgust some of my readers, but don't despair. You are not alone. Now that I am in the latter part of my life, I tend to agree. I don't even like to hunt now. I'm simply trying to tell you how it was when I was a young, adventurous country boy.

We successfully baited our hooks and eagerly cast them into the dark waters of the Big Log, hoping not to snag one of the underwater cypress knees. I cannot begin to tell you how exciting it was watching our corks being pulled around this way and that by roaches trying vainly to escape certain death. It was very different than watching a still, floating cork, waiting for it to tremble or dip down beneath the surface of the water.

Allen, who was always the best fisherman in our group, stood up quickly as his cork suddenly skidded across the creek and disappeared in the dark water. "I got one!" he shouted, his reed pole quivering and bending in the shape of a rainbow.

"Hold him tight!" I yelled as if he didn't know.

After expertly tugging his pole back and forth for several minutes, Allen wore the fish down and slowly dragged the fat, still struggling, jack to the bank of the creek.

"That's a fine one!" We both admired his catch and rushed to repeat the performance. We kept at it until our bucket was emptied of bait and filled with fresh, still breathing, jackfish, just waiting to be fried! The hot sun, now high in the sky, began to filter down through the cypress trees and pop out sweat on our brows. Finally, when a smart jackfish wrapped my fishing line around a cypress knee until the line snapped, we sighed and called it a day.

It was a happy sigh, and we accepted with pleasure the congratulations of the neighbors we passed on the way home. Allen even invented the story of the *big* one I snagged, so big that it snapped my line and got away. I suspect you may have heard that one.

CHAPTER TWENTY-THREE

White Thing

IT WAS LATE Saturday afternoon, and the sun was beginning to sink behind the tall pine trees. Dewey Lee, Brother, Thurston, Benjamin, Allen, and I, all Coopers, were at Uncle Dewey's as usual, sitting on the porch. We were becoming restless watching the descending sun sink low enough for us to begin our trek to the woods. Catfishing was always done at night. Catfish lay in the mud on the bottom of the creek during the day and came to the surface to search for food only after dark, which gave us an opportunity for an exciting nighttime camping adventure.

Normally we fished for catfish on Sapony Creek at the bottom of the Brinkley Hill, but during the afternoon we had decided to try the Cherry Hole, a pond of water in the Pine Forest located on the south side of Little Sapony behind Uncle Dewey's house.

We spent a fun afternoon getting ready. We dug for fishing worms, begged our parents for the usual strips of fat meat for emergency bait, strung our hooks and lines to our reed fishing poles, and attached our sinkers. Of course, our parents had to help with the food supplies, too. This was to be a real safari. One of us collected coffee in a paper sack and brought an empty can to boil the coffee. Others brought eggs to be boiled and biscuits to sustain us.

Of course, Mother, who always worried that I wouldn't have enough to eat, made ham sandwiches that were scorned initially by the gang. Ben said, "Tommy, on a camping trip we're supposed to cook our own food. We're old enough to take care of ourselves." I was embarrassed but kept the sandwiches anyway. Much later it was fun to hear them sheepishly apologize after greedily accepting my offered sandwiches on the bank of the Cherry Hole.

With all our supplies divided among us, we marched in single file from Uncle Dewey's backyard into the pine woods. By the time we reached the little footpath leading through the forest to the Cherry Hole, the sun seemed to have taken a nosedive. It was pitch dark except for the bright, shimmering stars that exploded throughout the sky and seemed to cover us with a blanket of diamonds. Ben, who was in front, stopped to light the lantern, but not before the rest of us bumped into each other, causing him to drop it. We all sat down on the edge of the path waiting for Ben to get us some light.

He cocked his head, and said, "Listen to that. It's the prettiest, most soothing piece of music you'll ever hear." We had already heard but hadn't really listened. Now we did. The July flies buzzing high up in the oak trees that dotted the pine forest, the crickets singing their tune everywhere, the occasional whippoorwill whistling his name, and the frogs croaking to us where they were: "under the root, under the root." It was and still is my favorite piece of music.

After a few minutes had elapsed, Allen stood up and said eagerly, "OK. Enough of this. Let's go on down to the Cherry Hole. You know, before we can go catfishing we've got to get a lot of things done. *Then* we can lay around the fire and talk as long as we want to."

The Cherry Hole was about a half mile down the path, and we talked all the way. As soon as we got there, we dropped our gear on the bank, and Benjamin began to get us organized.

"The first thing we need to do is gather some wood for the fire so we can see what we're doin'. Allen, you've got one lantern, so you and Tommy can go one way. Dewey Lee, you and Thurston can go another way, and Brother and I'll take the other lantern and go the other way. There're a lot of dead limbs on the ground. It hasn't rained in a good while so they should be dry."

Everybody agreed. Allen and I chose the area right next to the Cherry Hole. There were many dry limbs and a few small pine trees that had lost the race for the sun with the big tall pines. We dragged the limbs and tree trunks to the place where the fire was to be built. Allen and I actually enjoyed going back and forth gathering the firewood as the pile of wood grew quickly.

"We've got enough," Ben yelled. We all came to where we had built up a little pile of limbs and three tree trunks. "All we need now," he explained, "is a little pine straw, and we'll be ready to fire away. First, though, we got to brush the ground clear of pinecones, bark, and anything that could catch fire. We don't want any flames to escape and burn up the woods." Ben crammed the pine straw we had collected for the fire under the dry limbs and logs, and it wasn't long before a nice crackling blaze peeked through the smoke and quickly spread through our pile of brush. We were almost ready to start catching some fish.

Catfishing was different from any other kind of fishing, at least in my neck of the woods. Each of us baited two or three poles at the same time. Instead of standing and holding the pole until we got a bite the way we did fishing for perch, we stuck as many baited poles as we could watch into the bank as far apart as we wished and left them there unattended. As the night progressed we checked them from time to time, or left them overnight and returned early the next morning to collect our catch.

The most thrilling part to me was walking along the bank to see if any of my poles were shaking or being jerked around. If so, I would carefully pull the pole and gently lift to the bank a big, whiskered, yellow catfish with the hook firmly embedded in his lip. A sharp jerk of the line would have torn the hook out of his mouth and freed the fish, a sad end that we had learned to avoid. Of course if the line was perfectly still and stayed that way, I would pull it out of the water, usually to find an empty hook. Catfish were notoriously skilled at stealing bait.

By the time we had set our poles and returned to the campsite on this particular evening, the fire had illuminated a large area, enough for us to prepare our supper. With our eggs boiling in a coffee can, Ben, the official cook for the night, filled another can with water from the Cherry Hole and started boiling it before dropping in the loose coffee.

In a few minutes we had hard-boiled eggs that we immediately broke and shelled, applied a little salt and began munching as if we were a starving bunch of mice around a flour barrel in the pantry. With the eggs quickly devoured, Ben used a tightly woven sugar sack to strain the coffee into each of our cups. Although most of us did not drink coffee at home, here on the banks of the Cherry Hole, we were all grown men. We settled back, nibbling Mother's ham sandwiches and sipping our vile-tasting coffee, pretending that it was delicious. We began to talk.

"Ya know, this is the kind of life I like. Too bad it's comin' to an end," Dewey Lee sighed.

"Whadda you talkin' about?" Thurston glared at him. "It ain't endin!"

"It's almost September. Can anybody think of anything good or maybe bad that's happening in September?" Dewey Lee asked.

Everyone had a quizzical look until Allen yelled the dreaded word: "*School!*"

From there the conversation quickly lapsed into who hated which teacher, playing sick to escape the misery of going to school, or even skipping school altogether. That conversation finally ended with no answer to the dilemma, but with a general agreement that the summer vacation was coming to an end.

"Did y'all hear about the mad dog that bit the girl over near Spring Hope?" Ben began. Everybody started talking to each other, and Ben gave up.

Brother had better luck. The conversation quickly died down when in a soft, foreboding voice that compelled our immediate attention, he started telling us a story, a true story, he said, about the Cherry Hole.

"It was on a night like this that a bunch of grown men were at the Cherry Hole catfishing just like us and sittin' around the fire talkin' just like us when somethin' very, very strange happened."

Brother slowly lifted one hand and with a slightly trembling finger pointed. "You see that old tree there." Near the fire site was an old dead tree trunk that had fallen in the water, reaching nearly halfway across the Cherry Hole where it sank from view. No one could remember a time when that tree trunk wasn't there. It was so old it had almost petrified. "Well, you know it all happened on and around that same old tree trunk."

"What? What happened?" I questioned, my voice suddenly hoarse and, to my embarrassment, a little squeaky.

"Hush! Let him go on," Thurston urged.

"Well," Brother began to enjoy the attention. "Everybody around the fire was talkin' to one another when they heard a loud splashin' noise!

"One of the men said, 'Did you hear that big fish?'

"'Ain't no fish big enough to make that kinda splash,' his partner whispered, his eyes wide with fright. 'It came from the other side of the yellow log!'

"Everyone craned their necks trying to see what is was, but it won't any use. They couldn't see a thing. Two or three of the men ran to the other side of the log for a better view, and what they saw made them cry out, 'Good Lord!' 'What? What is it?' everybody asked at once, afraid to talk above a whisper. They got no answer.

"Then they all saw it climbin' from the other side to the top of the log. 'It's white all over and it keeps changing shapes,' someone shouted.

"'The thing has a head,' somebody else yelled.

"One of the other men, a lot braver than the rest, grabbed an ax and started runnin' toward the old tree trunk, screamin' at the top of his voice, 'I'm gonna git the white thing's head so we can all see what it is.' Then he jumped up on the tree trunk, swung the ax over his head and then down on the white thing, slicin' it in half. One half fell on one side of the log and the other on the other side. Everybody there cheered; the ax man took a bow.

"Everybody shouted, 'Let's see it! Let's see the white thing! Is it dead?' But then all the men went stone silent. All eyes stared at the white thing. One half of it swam out to the end of the log, and the other half swam out to meet it. Then the two halves joined together, and the white thing swam away.

"And that is the end of the story of the white thing," Brother concluded. "I wonder if it's still around here somewhere?"

"But what was it?" we all wanted to know.

"I don't know. I never heard anything but 'white thing.'" Brother shook his head.

We all just sat there in silence for a moment. Then somebody asked, "What did the men do then?"

"I'll tell you what they did," said Dewey Lee, suddenly jumping up. "They left just like I'm gonna do!"

"Not by yourself!" everybody chimed in, bumping into each other in their haste to get out of there, leaving everything. "We'll get all that and check the fishing poles in the morning!"

Of course the most enjoyable part of catfishing time was sitting around a campfire, drinking bad coffee, and telling ghost stories. But, somehow, after I heard the story of the white thing for the first time, fishing at the Cherry Hole was never quite the same again.

CHAPTER TWENTY-FOUR

Daddy

Daddy and the Neighbor

ONE SATURDAY AFTERNOON Daddy and I were sitting under the well shelter, sharpening weeding hoes that were in constant use for chopping grass out of the cotton and tobacco. Suddenly Daddy raised his head. "Hear that? That's Bison Matthews and Lizzie. Hear the wagon? It's coming up the hill ditches now," Daddy chuckled.

"Yeah, I hear it. Reckon Mr. Bison'll be driving Lizzie, or will it be the other way around?"

"Same old way," Daddy answered.

Well, it may be hard to believe, but the story I'm about to tell you is true. Bison Matthews, I'll call him, lived on a farm that was surrounded by thick woods. His only outlet to the public road was a little path that connected to the bigger path that went by our house. Every Saturday morning Bison would come by on his one-horse wagon, pulled by his mule Lizzie. When he passed on his way to Nashville, he never spoke or acknowledged that he had even seen us although we may have waved at him. In the neighborhood he was known to be a mean, curious, crabby old weekend drunk, and I now believe that going without alcohol during weekdays is what actually ruined his disposition.

When Mr. Bison, as everybody called him, went to town, he would always tie Old Lizzie to the hitching rack behind the poolroom. By 3 o'clock in the afternoon or sometimes earlier, he would get so drunk he would pass out completely. In those days everybody knew everybody, so whoever was around at the time would load Mr. Bison in the wagon, untie Old Lizzie and point her in the right direction. Then Old Lizzie, with no help from Mr. Bison lying unconscious in the back of the wagon, would plod her way the three or four miles along the road and then up the path by our house and beyond to his house.

On arrival, Old Lizzie would walk up to the stable and wait for some of Mr. Bison's children to carry him in the house, then unbridle her and turn her out to graze in the pasture, her weekend work completed successfully once again.

Whenever Daddy would see Old Lizzie carrying Mr. Bison home, he would say, "I see it, but I don't believe it." I still don't believe it, either, but it's true. I guess Old Lizzie was the very first designated driver.

One day, Daddy and I were cutting bushes that encroached in the open field on the boundary line between our farm and the farm owned by Mr. Bison. We were shocked to hear the gruff, yet shrill, voice of Mr. Bison, shouting out, "What in the hell do you think you're doing? You're on my property. Get off now."

Daddy, in a seemingly surprised voice, said, "Good gracious! I'm sorry. I didn't know. Let's go back and look at the iron stake line marker." This stake, of course, marked the property line between our farms.

We all walked back together to the iron marker, Mr. Bison cursing all the way. The iron stake was an old rusty pipe, embedded in the soil. You could tell it had not been moved in ages. It further showed that we were clearly on our property a foot or two off Mr. Bison's line.

I was stunned to hear Daddy say, "Bison, I'm sorry. I always thought this stob was on the line, but I'll pull it up. Then you can put it where you think the line is."

Well, believe it or not, Mr. Bison appeared to be more stunned than I was. After what seemed like five minutes, he spoke in a calm, embarrassed tone, "Hell, Roy, you might be right. Don't pull the dammed thing up." Without another word, he turned and slowly walked away.

I was dumbfounded. "Daddy, suppose he had said to pull it up and move it? What would you have done?"

Daddy answered, "I knew that he knew where the line stake was. He just felt bad this morning. He's not a mean man."

"How did you know all this?" I questioned, but Daddy never answered.

We went back to cutting bushes.

In later life I have wondered about this encounter. Daddy was not a Bible reader, so I don't think he had ever read Deuteronomy 19: 14, which admonishes us never to steal a man's land by moving the boundary marker. I guess he just instinctively knew what was right and wrong and how to deal with people fairly.

Daddy and My Education

IN THE DAYS before the use of fuel oil and before bulk tobacco barns had ever been heard of, Daddy and Mother had to tend the curing barns by using wood to fire the brick furnaces. On these days when Daddy was at the barn adjusting the temperature and regulating the heat to cure our tobacco crop in his usual expert fashion, he and I would have our most serious talks.

I have already written that my daddy was a man of few words, but you know I really believe he enjoyed our little private chats at the curing barn. Our subjects were about many topics of interest to a young country boy: animals that roamed our nearby woodlands, birds, flying squirrels, his adventures when he was a young man, and ghost stories. We ran the gamut.

But you may have guessed that the dominant theme of these conversations was the necessity of my going to college. These talks would always begin and end with Daddy's declaring, "Times have changed. In these times you'll amount to nothing unless you have a college education."

Sometimes when Daddy was not in a talkative mood, I could always get him started by jerking his chain, saying something like, "My friend James White misses many days of school. Why can't I?"

In a loud angry voice Daddy would begin the expected tirade with "Yes, but he won't be worth a cent! In this day and time a good education is a must, and that means college." He would continue in this vein for several minutes. Then, after recovering from his initial indignation at my senseless remark, he would usually lapse into a conversation much more to my liking.

Well, believe it or not, after a few years I really began to enjoy school. I will always thank my daddy for pushing me in the right direction to obtain a good education and for giving me the money to pay for it. Money was hard to come by in those days.

I remember one day in particular when I came home from Wake Forest College. I can see my daddy now, standing on the street corner in front of Gulley's Hardware in Nashville. Even though he was wearing a worn denim coat and overalls held up by sturdy galluses hung loosely over his shoulders, he was an imposing figure: tall, broad shoulders, muscular but slim, the result of years of tough farm labor. He had a handsome face, ruddy complexion, high cheekbones, and thick black hair, all of which convinced me there must have been an American Indian somewhere in our ancestry. He looked at me and said simply, "Need any money?"

I really needed two hundred dollars for books and food and other necessities of college life, but I couldn't bring myself to ask for all of it. Instead I said, "Well, I could use a hundred dollars." He took me straight across the street to Peoples' Bank, withdrew one hundred dollars and asked, "You sure that's enough?"

"A gracious plenty," I assured him. He was tight with his money, but never with me. I made do with what he generously gave me.

Uncle Bernard

IN LATER YEARS I wondered about Daddy's insistence on a college education for me and about his care in seeing that I had the money I needed. I have come to believe that his brother Bernard might have been at least partially responsible.

The union of James Pharoah Cooper and Lucy J. Baines produced eight children: four girls and four boys. Bernard Cooper was the oldest of the four boys, and Daddy was next in line. Daddy never mentioned Bernard's name unless someone asked about him, and his answer was always the same, a simple "yes," "no," or "I don't want to talk about it."

Well, on the day that I received my long-awaited acceptance letter from Wake Forest College, I immediately ran from the mailbox to find Mother and Daddy. Both of my parents were overcome with joy, as was I. We sat around and grinned at one another until finally Daddy stood up, saying, "I've got to go to the barns. Want to go with me?" Of course I did.

To my surprise, Daddy wanted to tell me Bernard's story. "On Bernard's first day in school," he began, "a whole new world opened up for him. It didn't take the teachers long to recognize that his intelligence level was way above the other students and probably of the teachers themselves. You know he never missed a day of school even when there was a big snow on the ground. If a teacher was absent, he was asked to teach the class.

"Books. Our little bedroom was filled with them. Bernard would spend every spare moment of his time reading. After he got all the schooling he could get at the little Deans School, he begged Papa for money to go to college. Papa didn't have any money, but he offered to give Bernard one acre of tobacco to use what money he could make, any way he wanted."

"Daddy, how could he get in college with so little time in school? Did he have to take an entrance exam?" I questioned.

"I don't know the answers to your questions, but, if there was any kind of test, he had no problem. Well, he went to Trinity College, I think they call it Duke now, for a short time. When he came back home, I could tell there was something wrong. He would stay up most of the night reading his books and then work all day trying to make enough money to go back to college for another term.

"One night I got up and looked over his shoulder. He was holding his book upside down. After that, things went from bad to worse. Finally no one could handle him except me, and I couldn't be with him all the time. He got so bad we had to send him to the mental asylum at Dix Hill where he has been ever since," Daddy ended with a deep sigh.

"Do you ever visit him?" I asked.

"Yes," he answered.

"How does he get along?"

Daddy said nothing further, and I knew the conversation about Bernard was over. He loved Bernard, I know, and I have often wondered if that experience influenced him in his insistence on my education and his generosity with his hard-earned money. He wanted to be sure I had the time and backing I needed to succeed. Bernard died on March 5, 1967, his 73rd birthday.

My daddy was such an interesting man that I treasured the times that I was with him; and, you know, though he never said so, I could tell that he liked being with me.

In writing these few words about my daddy, I realize anew how much his values are now my values, how greatly he influenced my life. From my observations, I do believe I have been successful in passing these standards on to my sons. He would be pleased.

After working all day in the field, Daddy relaxes on a slide truck of tobacco.

EPILOGUE

My grandchildren used to have a contraption that squeezed out something like clay in a variety of shapes, determined by their chosen molds.

As I think about my young life, I keep seeing that clay and am amazed to realize that I have not strayed far from the molds my parents, grandparents, and neighbors chose for me. I have added my own unique bits and pieces here and there, but I see in these stories the basics of my adult self.

My parents never read a book on child psychology or parenting techniques. Where did they get the molds which so clearly shaped my life? The answer is, of course, from *their* parents, grandparents, and neighbors. Just as Beverly and I, our parents, neighbors and friends in turn have shaped our children. The basics have remained the same, with each generation adding its own twist.

Writing *Between the Creeks* has helped me understand as never before what the Cooper family tradition is all about: love of God and family, integrity, community service, hard work, and insistence on quality education. I know that may sound like bragging, but I'm proud of my family. I do know I'll have to keep being careful not to let the clay dry and crack around the edges as it ages. There are more molds to cast.

ACKNOWLEDGMENTS

FIRST AND FOREMOST I want to thank my Elm Grove Community neighbors and friends, living and dead, for making my young life memorable and for instilling in me the values that have made my life meaningful. I thank God that I have been privileged to live between the creeks with family, close friends, and nature at its finest.

As a matter of fact, there doesn't seem to be a stopping point for my memories. We haven't even mentioned the story of the weasel in the barn or the owl in the hog pen, nor have I told you of the joy of tracking rabbits on a snowy morning.

The stories you have read actually happened and are vivid in my mind, but I may have gotten a name wrong here and there. I know you understand.

I want to express my great sense of loss that my cousin Grover Cooper died unexpectedly in February 2007, and that he is not here to enjoy with me the publication of my first book. An author himself, Grover encouraged me to try my hand at writing.

As to the actual writing, editing, and publication of my adventures, I could never have completed this project without the untiring and skillful efforts of my wife, Beverly; my children, Roy and Pell; and our dear friend, Julia White.

In addition, I want to express my appreciation to Edwina Woodbury and Katie Severa of Chapel Hill Press, Inc., for their unfailing patience and expert guidance in the publication of this book.